Real Estate Exam Prep (PSI)

The Authoritative Guide to Preparing for the PSI General Exam

Third Edition

John R. Morgan

On-The-Test Publishing
(www.On-the-Test.com)

ISBN-13   978-0-9711941-3-7
ISBN-10   0-9711941-3-0

Published by:

On-The-Test Publishing
Post Office Box 231
Waterford, Connecticut 06385
www.On-the-Test.com
email: PSIBook@On-the-Test.com

We welcome reader comments and suggestions about our text and test questions.
Please contact the publisher at the email address above regarding either.
Email us about typos, terms, and omissions in this book,
as well as your thoughts on useful inclusions in future printings.
We especially welcome hearing how your understanding of topics was enhanced and your
test-confidence -- and success!-- was ensured by anything in this book.

Dedication

This edition is dedicated to Elaine "Grammy" Walsh,
without whom I would have not had the lakeside and oceanfront writer's retreats
that have provided idyllic surroundings while I work to keep these volumes updated.

Many thanks.

Publisher's Foreword

With few exceptions, state real estate licensing agencies contract with a company specializing in examination administration services to administer tests for their licensing candidates. These companies typically offer test development services as well, and have prepared an exam known variously as a "uniform," "national," or "general" exam and follow it with a shorter exam that is state-specific.

General exams are designed to test subject matter that is common across state lines, and to specifically avoid testing terms, concepts, practices, and laws that are either regional or state-specific in nature: those topics are usually tested in the state-specific portion of the exam. This book covers just the general portion of the exam.

Psychological Services, Inc. (PSI), a company based in Burbank, California, has been a provider of real estate licensing examination services for nearly two decades and is becoming increasingly more sensitive to national applicability of specific terms, concepts, and practices as its client roster grows nationwide.

General exams prepared by test vendors are reviewed for adherence to a comprehensive set of guidelines for test development by the Association of Real Estate License Law Officials (ARELLO®). PSI's exams have been repeatedly accredited by ARELLO®'s Examination Accreditation Program.

For more information on ARELLO®, which has links to the websites of state licensing agencies nationwide, PSI, and other vendors that may have information on a non-PSI-client state of interest to you, especially Candidate Information Brochures with state-specific examination and licensing information, visit the following websites:

- *www.arello.org* for information about ARELLO® as well as state links
- *www.psiexams.com* for information on PSI and its client states
- *www.goamp.com* for information on *AL, GA, IL, MI, MO, MT, NE, NH, ND, SD, VT, WA, and WY*
- *www.pearsonvue.com* for information on *AK, AR, AZ, DE, DC, FL, ID, IN, KS, KY, ME, MA, RI, TX, UT, and WI*

(Note: states occasionally change exam vendors, so check the other vendor websites if you cannot find the state you are looking for at the one given.)

The publisher wishes to make these final important clarifications:

Nothing in this publication should be construed as indicating PSI's endorsement of, involvement in, or responsibility for any of the author's interpretations, elaborations, or commentary on the PSI general content outline's list of commonplace real estate topics.

All interpretations of and elaborations on real estate subject matter and are based on close research of standard texts, legal reference works, state-specific curriculum guides, and government websites, along with editorial recommendations from a nationwide group of reviewers in the fields of real estate regulation, law, practice, and instruction.

All opinions regarding testing practices, policies, or procedures are those of the author based primarily on his professional test development training at the Educational Testing Service (ETS) and subsequent application of that training to real estate licensing programs in over twenty states and the Government of Bermuda. They are not necessarily shared currently by PSI, ARELLO®, or any other organization named in this text.

Author's Introduction to the General Exam Review

As a real estate student or instructor, some of the prelicensing textbook material you study makes you ask yourself that age-old question, "Will this be on the test?"

On-the-Test: Real Estate books address that question through a concentrated, no-nonsense approach that will prepare you more effectively, ***in under 140 pages***, than other general-prep books do with more than twice the number of pages—and additional required reading time!

To begin with, consider the PSI exam content outline: It begins where you are, with learning basic real estate terminology and concepts of property ownership, rights, and control in Sections I and II, following these essential basics with terms, concepts, and processes common to valuation in Section III.

Section IV concentrates on the broad range of details involved in financing a property transaction, while Sections V and VI cover those terms, concepts, principles, processes, and requirements applicable to common-law agency relationships as they relate to real estate transactions.

These are followed by Sections VII and VIII, which brings you where most successful real estate transactions go: to contractual relationships between parties, including purchase-and-sale agreements, and a property closing with a host of documents being prepared, explained, signed, and recorded.

Section IX supplements elements of Sections V, VI, and VII by separating out the terminology and requirements specified in federal Fair Housing law as well as advertising requirements found in the federal Truth in Lending Act (Regulation Z) and other important laws, conventions, and practices.

Section X clusters math computation questions commonly performed for various steps in a real estate transaction, and Section XI identifies and discusses several important real estate areas that do not always fit easily in ordinary sales-related transactions.

This book will build on the logical flow of the outline to clarify what you need to know in each of the outline's Topic Areas. As I have considered which terms and concepts are most logically associated with each area, I have addressed them with the following principles in mind.

1. **Exam outline-area organization of key terms and concepts**
   - This means like-terms are clustered where they are most likely to be categorized for test use, regardless of where they may appear in a standard textbook presentation.
2. **Question-count indication of relative importance of each outline Topic Area**
   - This should lessen anxiety about having to know *everything* in a particular Topic Area, since you will know that there may be just a few – perhaps no – questions from it.
3. **Concise, direct definitions and descriptions**
   - This avoids over-explanation, especially where further elaboration could detract from the central, testable content. This book provides a focused review of textbook material. If you want more words, refer to your main textbook.
4. **Synonymous terms are presented together as "extra" terms**
   - This clarifies, as often as possible, that similar terms are, in fact, synonymous, and the way your textbook presented a topic may be tested by PSI with another term.
5. **Bold-faced and italicized identification of terms, definitions, and key phrases**
   - This serves to accentuate the more important content within a description or general statement. These formats will also highlight terms that may be used as *wrong answers*, known as "***distractors***" in the education and testing businesses, so unfamiliar terms will not trick you into thinking, "I should have studied that!"

Author's Introduction to the General Exam Review

6. **Related _nontestable_ information is included, usually boldfaced and/or italicized**
   - This allows you to see more advanced, obscure, or regional information in the cluster of related material that, though inappropriate for testing, may appear as distractors.

7. **Italicized commentary**
   - This allows me to provide occasional conversational asides intended to further clarify a point, reduce potential topic-related anxiety, or stress nontestable topics.

8. **Minimal math emphasis**
   - This low emphasis is based on the less-than 8% emphasis of math on the exam, which makes math-related questions important, but not critical to one's overall score.

     This author is unapologetic about leaving math instruction to your 500+ page textbook: Enough of the math questions on the live exam will be basic enough to be easy. (A test-wise tip for those with weak math skills or high math anxiety is to compensate by becoming stronger in other areas.)

9. **Sufficient, not excessive, numbers of sample questions, and diagnostic chart**
   - The questions presented at the end of this book address central and critical topics adequately rather than exhaustively. The Sample Exam corresponds more closely to PSI's published outline specifications than any you will find by other authors, and the diagnostic chart allows you to check your exam-readiness.

As noted on the cover, this book is designed with **_both students and instructors_** in mind.

- **Prelicensing students** will find it useful as a concise, comprehensive presentation of textbook principles and practices material in a test-outline format. And, since it distills the key terms and concepts presented in most standard texts, its usefulness will continue once you are licensed by serving as light, handy, quick-reference book!
- **Instructors** will find it a ready-made manual for a highly focused and effectively concentrated end-of-course review.

My only direct experience with PSI's general examination came by taking it in the spring of 1999 to earn my Connecticut salesperson license. Through this exposure, I became convinced that the item pools PSI uses for its exams provide an adequate, well-crafted sampling of the content domain of real estate.

So, sorry: There are no shocking secrets to be revealed about "questions to watch out for." And no, "C" is not the most frequent answer, or the best bet for guessing: testing companies strive for an even mix.

Instead, everything herein is based on well-reasoned consideration and a unique perspective on which real estate terms and concepts are most appropriately suggested by the published outline headings.

Further, my involvement with Assessment Systems, Inc. (ASI)'s fully national Real Estate Job Analysis along with a close review of the follow-up ASI Job Analysis Technical Report (1998), many state-specific prelicensing course outlines, and numerous real estate and legal texts support the inclusion of the key words, topics, and distractors presented in this book.

My confidence that this book is the best one available rests primarily on my belief that the direct, concise presentation and organization of this text is grounded in unparalleled experience with real estate licensing examination subject matter and Subject Matter Experts nationwide.

So, knowing what dozens of committees of Subject Matter Experts have concluded during review sessions does give me a refined sense of what would pass muster. And soon when _you_ see a strange term and wonder, "Will this be on the test?" you, too, will know **_exactly_** what to say!

Acknowledgments

Thanks go to the many educators and regulators who have encouraged me to write this book.

By providing a concise reference to both real estate subject matter and how it is tested, I hope it serves their goals of continuing to strengthen and improve both real estate instruction and professional real estate test development programs nationwide.

In addition, many, many thanks to all of the regulators, instructors, and practitioners I've worked with in many high-spirited and highly productive test development meetings nationwide and since going independent, in Bermuda. Every meeting was an adventure and a success. Then, and even more now, I appreciate what Tom Samph, co-founder and longtime president of Assessment Systems, Inc. (ASI), said when I asked him what he missed most about life "after" ASI:

"The clients. They're what it's all about."

So, I would like to thank, at least by reference, everyone who contributed their time to improving their state exams and in doing so helped me hone my skills regarding testable real estate content.

Thanks go to every client and committee member I met with in:
Alaska, Arizona, Arkansas, Colorado, Delaware, the District of Columbia, Hawaii, Illinois, Indiana, Kansas, Kentucky, Massachusetts, Minnesota, New Jersey, Pennsylvania, Rhode Island, South Carolina, Tennessee, Utah, and Washington.

These committees constantly drove home the importance of asking questions drawn from current real estate information, processes, and practices that were both appropriate and relevant for entry-level real estate professionals. The distinction they observed between "need to know versus nice to know" generally weeded out weak, too-advanced, too-detailed, or irrelevant questions during periodic, routine committee reviews of both existing and newly written test questions.

They were painstakingly conscientious in setting expectations for entry-level performance while identifying significant details licensees will learn after entering the business. Further, they duly noted numerous transaction-related topics and details that other professionals, especially lawyers, lenders, appraisers, and accountants, are more appropriately responsible for knowing.

This book aspires to do justice to their example of discussing much more than would be on the test while respecting the line between what is testable and what is also important to know.

This edition incorporates routine updates along with enhanced treatment of some of the General-exam sections based on PSI's 2009 "expanded" outline, which identifies 171 sub-topics that stretches to three pages the previous one-page "concise" version.

Many general refinements are grounded in elegantly nuanced editorial observations offered by Charlie Wyatt, who founded and still teaches at South Carolina's longest-operating real estate school. I am grateful for his generosity in sharing his sharp-eyed insights and real estate expertise and thank him on behalf of the beneficiaries of his persuasive comments: the readers of this book.

I apologize in advance to the same readers for any deficiencies and oversights that remain—they are solely my doing.

Real Estate Exam: PSI's General Content Outline
Concise Version *(Version with Sub-Topics Begins on Next Page)*
80 questions for both Sales and Broker exams
There are 6 math-related questions; this represents a 7.5% overall math emphasis.
*(Your exam **may** also include an extra five unscored "pretest" questions for a total of 85.)*

I—Property Ownership   (7 questions)
- A. Classes of Property
- B. Land Characteristics and Legal Descriptions
- C. Encumbrances and Effects on Property Ownership
- D. Types of Ownership

II—Land Use Controls and Regulations   (5 questions)
- A. Government Rights in Land
- B. Public Controls Based in Police Power
- C. Regulation of Environmental Hazards
- D. Private Controls

III—Valuation and Market Analysis   (8 questions)
- A. Value
- B. Methods of Estimating Value/Appraisal Process
- C. Competitive/Comparative Market Analysis (CMA)
- D. Appraisal Practice; Situations Requiring Appraisal by a Certified Appraiser

IV—Financing   (6 questions)
- A. General Concepts
- B. Types of Loans and Sources of Loan Money
- C. Government Programs
- D. Mortgages/Deeds of Trust
- E. Financing/Credit Laws

V—General Principles of Agency   (10 questions)
- A. Nature of Agency Relationships
- B. Creation and Disclosure of Agency and Agency Agreements (General) *[Regulatory Details in State Portion]*
- C. Responsibilities of Agent/Principal
- D. Responsibilities of Agent to Customers and Third Parties, including Disclosure, Honesty, Integrity, Accounting for Money
- E. Termination of Agency

VI—Property Condition and Disclosures   (8 questions)
- A. Property Condition Disclosure
- B. Warranties
- C. Need for Inspection and Obtaining/Verifying Information
- D. Material Facts Related to Property Condition or Location
- E. Material Facts Related to Public Controls, Statutes, or Public Utilities

VII—Contracts   (11 questions)
- A. General Knowledge of Contract Law
- B. Listing Agreements
- C. Buyer/Tenant Representation Agreements, including Key Elements and Provisions of Buyer and/or Tenant Agreements
- D. Offers/Purchase Agreements
- E. Counteroffers/Multiple Counteroffers
- F. Leases
- G. Other Real Estate Contracts

VIII—Transfer of Title   (5 questions)
- A. Title Insurance
- B. Deeds
- C. Escrow or Closing; Tax Aspects of Transferring Title to Real Property
- D. Special Processes

IX—Practice of Real Estate   (12 questions)
- A. Trust/Escrow Accounts (General) *[Regulatory Details in State Portion]*
- B. Federal Fair Housing Laws
- C. Advertising and Technology
- D. Agent Supervision and Broker-Associate Relationship
- E. Commissions and Fees
- F. General Ethics
- G. Antitrust Laws

X—Real Estate Calculations   (6 questions)
- A. Basic Math Concepts
- B. Calculations for Transactions, including Mortgage Calculations
- C. Property Tax Calculations
- D. Prorations (Utilities, Rent, Property Taxes, Insurance, etc.)
- E. Calculations for Valuation

XI—Specialty Areas   (2 questions)
- A. Subdivisions, including Development-wide CC&Rs
- B. Commercial, Industrial, and Income Property

Note: There may be a few minor differences between the outline Topic Area labels above and those in the current PSI Bulletin. Any such difference in no way affects either the subject matter on the test or its presentation in this book.

Additionally, this outline specifically excludes the occasional one-or-two question difference in questions-per-Section for Broker exams.

Nevertheless, *the material in this book will more than adequately prepare those reviewing for a Broker exam*, which may test some of the terms identified herein as too advanced for Sales-level.

Real Estate Exam: PSI's General Content Outline
Expanded, Published Version Identifying 170 Sub-Topics
80 questions for both Sales and Broker exams
There are 6 math-related questions; this represents a 7-1/2% overall math emphasis.

I—Property Ownership   (7 questions)
- A. Classes of Property
    1. *Real versus Personal Property*
    2. *Defining Fixtures*
- B. Land Characteristics and Legal Descriptions
    1. *Physical Characteristics of Land*
    2. *Economic Characteristics of Land*
    3. *Types of Legal Property Descriptions*
    4. *Usage of Legal Property Descriptions*
    5. *Physical Description of Property and Improvements*
    6. *Mineral, Air, and Water Rights*
- C. Encumbrances and Effects on Property Ownership
    1. *Liens (Types and Priority)*
    2. *Easements and Licenses*
    3. *Encroachments*
- D. Types of Ownership
    1. *Types of Estates*
    2. *Forms of Ownership*
    3. *Leaseholds*
    4. *Common Interest Ownership Properties*
    5. *Bundle of Rights*

II—Land Use Controls and Regulations   (5 questions)
- A. Government Rights in Land
    1. *Property Taxes and Special Assessments*
    2. *Eminent Domain, Condemnation, Escheat*
    3. *Police Power*
- B. Public Controls Based in Police Power
    1. *Zoning and Master Plans*
    2. *Building Codes*
    3. *Environmental Impact Reports*
    4. *Regulation of Special Land Types (floodplain, coastal, etc.)*
- C. Regulation of Environmental Hazards
    1. *Abatement, Mitigation, and Cleanup Requirements*
    2. *Restrictions on Sale or Development of Contaminated Property*
    3. *Types of Hazards and Potential for Agent or Seller Liability*
- D. Private Controls
    1. *Deed Conditions or Restrictions for Specific Properties*
    2. *Homeowners Association (HOA) Regulations*

III—Valuation and Market Analysis   (8 questions)
- A. Value
    1. *Market Value and Market Price*
    2. *Value*
        a. *Types and Characteristics of Value*
        b. *Principles of Value*
        c. *Market Cycles and Other Factors Affecting Property Value*
- B. Methods of Estimating Value/Appraisal Process
    1. *Market or Sales Comparison Approach*
    2. *Replacement Cost or Summation Approach*
    3. *Income Approach*
    4. *Basic Appraisal Terminology (e.g. Replacement versus Reproduction Cost, Reconciliation, Depreciation, Kinds of Obsolescence)*

- C. Competitive/Comparative Market Analysis (CMA)
    1. *Selecting and Adjusting Comparables*
    2. *Contrast CMA and Appraisal*
        a. *Price per Square Foot*
        b. *Gross Rent and Gross Income Multipliers*
        c. *Capitalization Rate*
- D. Appraisal Practice; Situations Requiring Appraisal by Certified Appraiser

IV—Financing   (6 questions)
- A. General Concepts
    1. *LTV Ratios, Points, Origination Fees, Discounts, Broker Commissions*
    2. *Mortgage Insurance (PMI)*
    3. *Lender Requirements, Equity, Qualifying Buyers, Loan Application Procedures*
- B. Types of Loans and Sources of Loan Money
    1. *Term or Straight Loans*
    2. *Amortized and Partially Amortized (Balloon) Loans*
    3. *Adjustable Rate Mortgage (ARM) Loans*
    4. *Conventional versus Insured*
    5. *Reverse Mortgages, Equity Loans, Subprime and Other Nonconforming Loans*
    6. *Seller/Owner Financing*
    7. *Primary Market*
    8. *Secondary Market*
    9. *Down Payment Assistance Programs*
- C. Government Programs
    1. *FHA*
    2. *VA*
    3. *Other Federal Programs*
- D. Mortgages/Deeds of Trust
    1. *Mortgage Clauses (Assumption, Due-on-Sale, Alienation, Acceleration, Prepayment, Release)*
    2. *Lien Theory versus Title Theory*
    3. *Mortgage/Deed of Trust and Note as Separate Documents*
- E. Financing/Credit Laws
    1. *Lending and Disclosures*
        a. *Truth in Lending*
        b. *RESPA*
        c. *Integrated Disclosure Rule (TRID)*
        d. *Equal Credit Opportunity*
    2. *Fraud and Lending Practices*
        a. *Mortgage Fraud*
        b. *Predatory Lending Practices (Risks to Clients)*
        c. *Usury Lending Laws*
        d. *Appropriate Cautions to Clients Seeking Financing*

V—General Principles of Agency   (10 questions)
- A. Nature of Agency Relationships
    1. *Types of Agents and Agencies (Special, General, Designated, Subagent, etc.)*
    2. *Nonagents (Transactional/Facilitational)*
    3. *Fiduciary Responsibilities*

Real Estate Exam: PSI's General Content Outline
Expanded, Published Version Identifying 170 Sub-Topics
80 questions for both Sales and Broker exams
There are 6 math-related questions; this represents a 7-1/2% overall math emphasis.

B. Creation and Disclosure of Agency and Agency Agreements (General) *[Regulatory Details in State Portion]*
   1. *Agency and Agency Agreements*
   2. *Disclosure When Acting as Principal or other Conflict of Interest*
C. Responsibilities of Agent/Principal
   1. *Duties to Client/Principal (Buyer, Seller, Tenant, or Landlord)*
   2. *Traditional Common Law Agency Duties; Effect of Dual Agency on Agent's Duties*
D. Responsibilities of Agent to Customers and Third Parties, including Disclosure, Honesty, Integrity, Accounting for Money
E. Termination of Agency
   1. *Expiration*
   2. *Completion/Performance*
   3. *Termination by Force of Law*
   4. *Destruction of Property/Death of Principal*
   5. *Mutual Agreement*

VI—Property Condition and Disclosures   (8 questions)
A. Property Condition Disclosure
   1. *Property Owner's Role Regarding Property Condition*
   2. *Licensee's Role Regarding Property Condition*
B. Warranties
   1. *Purpose of Home or Construction Warranty Programs*
   2. *Scope of Home or Construction Warranty Programs*
C. Need for Inspection and Obtaining/Verifying Information
   1. *Explanation of Property Inspection Process and Appropriate Use*
   2. *Agent Responsibility to Inquire About "Red Flag" Issues*
   3. *Responding to Non-Client Inquiries*
D. Material Facts Related to Property Condition or Location
   1. *Land/Soil Conditions*
   2. *Accuracy of Representation of Lot or Improvement Size, Encroachments or Easements Affecting Use*
   3. *Pest Infestation, Toxic Mold, and other Interior Environmental Hazards*
   4. *Structural Issues such as Roof, Gutters, Downspouts, Doors, Windows, Foundation*
   5. *Condition of Electrical and Plumbing Systems, and of Equipment or Appliances that are Fixtures*
   6. *Location within Natural Hazard or Specifically Regulated Area, Potentially Uninsurable Property*
   7. *Known Alterations or Additions*
E. Material Facts Related to Public Controls, Statutes, or Public Utilities
   1. *Zoning and Planning Information*
   2. *Boundaries of School/Utility/Taxation Districts, Flight Paths*
   3. *Local Taxes and Special Assessments, Other Liens*
   4. *External Environmental Hazards*
   5. *Stigmatized/Psychologically Impacted Property, Megan's Law Issues*

VII—Contracts   (11 questions)
A. General Knowledge of Contract Law
   1. *Requirements for Validity*
   2. *When Contract is Considered Performed/ Discharged*
   3. *Assignment and Novation*
   4. *Breach of Contract and Remedies for Breach*
   5. *Contract Clauses*
B. Listing Agreements
   1. *General Requirements for Valid Listing*
   2. *Exclusive Listings*
   3. *Non-Exclusive Listings*
C. Buyer/Tenant Representation Agreements, including Key Elements and Provisions of Buyer and/or Tenant Agreements
D. Offers/Purchase Agreements
   1. *General Requirements*
   2. *When Offer Becomes Binding (Notification)*
   3. *Contingencies*
   4. *Time is of the Essence*
E. Counteroffers/Multiple Counteroffers
   1. *Counteroffer Cancels Original Offer*
   2. *Priority of Multiple Counteroffers*
F. Leases
   1. *Types of Leases, e.g., Percentage, Gross, Net, Ground*
   2. *Lease with Obligation to Purchase or Lease with an Option to Purchase*
G. Other Real Estate Contracts
   1. *Options*
   2. *Right of First Refusal*

VIII—Transfer of Title   (5 questions)
A. Title Insurance
   1. *What is Insured Against*
   2. *Title Searches, Title Abstracts, Chain of Title*
   3. *Cloud on Title, Suit to Quiet Title*
B. Deeds
   1. *Purpose of Deed, when Title Passes*
   2. *Types of Deeds (General Warranty, Special Warranty, Quitclaim) and When Used*
   3. *Essential Elements of Deeds*
   4. *Importance of Recording*
C. Escrow or Closing; Tax Aspects of Transferring Title to Real Property
   1. *Responsibilities of Escrow Agent*
   2. *Prorated Items*
   3. *Closing Statements/HUD-1*
   4. *Estimating Closing Costs*
   5. *Property and Income Taxes*
D. Special Processes
   1. *Foreclosure/Short Sale*
   2. *Real Estate Owned (REO)*

IX—Practice of Real Estate   (12 questions)
A. Trust/Escrow Accounts (General) *[Regulatory Details in State Portion]*
   1. *Purpose and Definition of Trust Accounts, including Monies Held in Trust Accounts*
   2. *Responsibility for Earnest Money and Other Trust Monies, including Commingling/Conversion*

Real Estate Exam: PSI's General Content Outline
Expanded, Published Version Identifying 170 Sub-Topics
80 questions for both Sales and Broker exams
There are 6 math-related questions; this represents a 7-1/2% overall math emphasis.

B. Federal Fair Housing Laws
1. *Protected Classes*
   a. *Covered Transactions*
   b. *Specific Laws and their Effects*
2. *Compliance*
   a. *Types of Violations and Enforcement*
   b. *Exceptions*
C. Advertising and Technology
1. *Incorrect "Factual" Statements versus "Puffing"*
   a. *Truth in Advertising*
   b. *Fair Housing Issues in Advertising*
2. *Fraud, Technology Issues*
   a. *Uninformed Misrepresentation versus Deliberate Misrepresentation (Fraud)*
   b. *Technology Issues in Advertising and Marketing*
D. Agent Supervision and Broker-Associate Relationship
1. *Liability/Responsibility for Acts of Associated Licensees (Employees or Independent Contractors) and Unlicensed Employees*
2. *Responsibility to Train and Supervise Associated Licensees (Employees or Independent Contractors) and Unlicensed Employees*
E. Commissions and Fees
1. *Procuring Cause/Protection Clauses*
2. *Referrals and Other Finder Fees*
F. General Ethics
1. *Practicing Within Area of Competence*
2. *Avoiding Unauthorized Practice of Law*
G. Antitrust Laws
1. *Antitrust Laws and Purpose*
2. *Antitrust Violations in Real Estate*

X—Real Estate Calculations   (6 questions)
A. Basic Math Concepts
1. *Area*
2. *Loan-to-Value Ratios*
3. *Discount Points*
4. *Equity*
5. *Down Payment/Amount to be Financed*
B. Calculations for Transactions, including Mortgage Calculations
C. Property Tax Calculations
D. Prorations (Utilities, Rent, Property Taxes, Insurance, etc.)
1. *Commission and Commission Splits*
2. *Seller's Proceeds of Sale*
3. *Transfer Tax/Conveyance Tax/Revenue Stamps*
4. *Amortization Tables*
5. *Interest Rates*
6. *Interest Amounts*
7. *Monthly Installment Payments*
8. *Buyer Qualification Ratios*
E. Calculations for Valuation
1. *Competitive/Comparative Market Analyses (CMA)*
2. *Net Operating Income*
3. *Depreciation*
4. *Capitalization Rate*
5. *Gross Rent and Gross Income Multipliers (GRM, GIM)*

XI—Specialty Areas   (2 questions)
A. Subdivisions, including Development-wide CC&Rs
B. Commercial, Industrial, and Income Property
1. *Trade Fixtures*
2. *Accessibility*
3. *Tax Depreciation*
4. *1031 Exchanges*
5. *Trust Fund Accounts for Income Property*

Note: There may be a few minor differences between the outline Topic Area labels above and those in the current PSI Bulletin. Any such difference in no way affects either the subject matter on the test or its presentation in this book.

Additionally, this outline specifically excludes the occasional difference of one or two questions per Section for Broker exams.

Nevertheless, *the material in this book will more than adequately prepare those reviewing for a Broker exam*, which may test some of the terms identified herein as too advanced for Sales-level.

Comments on PSI's "Expanded" Outline

Since mid-2009, PSI has been publishing an "expanded" outline in its Candidate Information Bulletins (CIBs); PSI outlines use to be more streamlined, using 11 Content Areas each with 5-10 Topic Areas.

PSI's current outline provides 170 sub-topics, which makes it substantially longer than PSI's original outlines—it is now six columns spread over three pages compared to one-and-a-half columns that typically fit on the same page. (For your convenience, we presented a "concise" outline on page viii that makes it easier to get an at-a-glance overview of the exam content, much like earlier PSI outlines.)

At first blush, an "expanded" outline makes the exam itself seem massive. But taking a step back shows that PSI's design has been to present an outline that illustrates and reinforces the real estate industry's belief that the profession requires robust, ever-changing applications of an enormous knowledge base to an extensive variety of both routine and innovative tasks. Further, instructors and students alike find useful guidance by seeing relevant sub-topics listed under the umbrella of broad Topic Area headings.

Unavoidably, such detail risks looking like it is exhaustive in itemizing what is 'in-bounds' for testing, and that if a term or topic is not found here, it cannot be fair game for use on the test.

However, this is just not so: the sub-topics *do not* definitively limit the scope of content coverage.

For example, in Topic Area IV-F, Financing/Credit Laws, TILA, RESPA, and ECOA are listed while Regulation Z, the Fair Credit Reporting Act, and the Private Mortgage Insurance (PMI) Act are not.

It would be remiss of any testing company to send the message that these are either unimportant laws or off-limits for testing, and I am confident that PSI not only recognizes their importance, but assembles some exams using questions on these topics rather than testing solely on the others.

This expanded outline is a progressive, instruction-friendly step for PSI, which in its own CIBs' "Tips for Preparing for Your Licensing Examination," specifically states that students should "use the examination content outline as the basis of your study."

In finally making some of the essential sub-topics explicit for students, PSI is attempting to help facilitate, not frustrate, pre-examination review of textbook and other pre-license course material.

Now when students—and instructors—wonder "What do they mean by 'Financing/Credit Laws,'" PSI provides at least a partial reply that offers *some* guidance about what to study.

As previously noted, PSI's examinations routinely undergo review by the ARELLO® Examination Accreditation Program, which has standards for determining what is testable and how test vendors can stay in-bounds. The following excerpts from its guidelines will support many of the comments you will find throughout this book regarding subject matter or terms that are either too-advanced, obscure, or insignificant, and are therefore not fair game for testing.

> Among ARELLO®'s question-writing guidelines are standards that for each question, the "subject matter being tested . . . must be **relevant and appropriate**" and "must be based on an **important** point, idea, or skill that reflects an appropriate level of competency in knowledge or skill related to tasks shown to be needed for entry level" *(ARELLO®'s emphasis)*.

So, despite the appearance of complexity presented by the overwhelmingly extensive array of sub-topics, PSI's expanded outline—and this book—simply helps students stay on-track while using "the examination content outline as the basis of . . . study."

Now it's time to begin the adventure!

Table of Contents

[This page intentionally left blank]

I-A. Classes of Property (Expect 1-2 questions from this area)

Real property, or **realty**, is **land along with its improvements**, things attached to it, and the benefits, rights, and interests included in its ownership.

> *Real property and real estate are well acknowledged as synonymous terms. However, "real property" is generally the preferred usage whenever it helps distinguish specific types of property as real instead of personal by avoiding the word "estate," which, in its broadest sense, means everything one owns, including both real and personal property.*

> As will be noted in Topic Area I-B, **land** includes the **earth's surface, subsurface to the center of the earth, the space overhead**, and **the rights to each**.

> **Improvements** are generally seen as additions to the property that increase its value or enhance its appearance and may include attached property, such as a house, garage, or fixtures like sinks or built-in bookcases, as well as trees and landscaping improvements.

> > *The opposite of improvements is **waste**, which is the legal term for property deterioration, abuse, or destruction, generally by a negligent tenant.*

Personal property, also known as **personalty** or **chattel**, is generally considered anything that is **unattached and moveable**, such as furniture, housewares, lawn mowers, and throw rugs.

> *Personal property also includes various **intangible assets**, like **bank accounts**, **stocks**, and many other **securities and financial instruments**.*

Fixtures are **once-moveable items that have been attached to real property**. Since attaching the object *may* change its status from personal to real property, as with a sink, a ceiling fan, or even a coat hook screwed to the back of a door, tenants and those selling their property must be careful about how they install items they may want to take away with them.

> **Trade fixtures** are fixtures used by a business tenant, such as display cases or supermarket freezers, that are generally considered the tenant's removable personal property.

> > **Annexation** is the term for how, by attachment, something that was formerly personal property becomes real property. Also referred to as **accession**, which includes additions to property from natural causes, such as a riverfront property that benefits from a shift in the river's path.

> > **Severance** refers to the process of separating a fixture from the real property, thereby changing it *from real to personal* property.

The legal tests for a fixture include considering the total circumstances of these four elements to determine whether or not the fixture is real or removable property
1. **intention** of the person who attached the item to make it permanent
2. **method of attachment**, or **annexation**, generally meaning the degree of permanence
3. **adaptation** of the item to the use of the property, as in a custom-made bookshelf that fits precisely into a recessed area and is attached with bolts

> **4. relationship and general understanding** between parties, as in whether the owner
> paid for and installed the fixture, or a tenant has done so at the tenant's expense with the
> owner's permission to remove it later

Appurtenances are those things that "belong" to something else, generally by ***attachment***, and in real estate generally include any number of rights that "***run with the land***," which means the rights do not end when a new owner takes title. Examples of these are gardens, buildings, and certain ***easements***, such as deeded rights-of-way. *(More in Topic Area I-C.)*

Emblements are crops that a tenant generally owns as personal property and may return to harvest even after a lease expires.

> *Growing crops are technically referred to as **fructus industriales** ("fruits of industry"),*
> *which distinguishes them from other plants, **fructus naturales** ("fruits of nature"), such as*
> *trees and brush, which are generally considered real property.*

> *These terms are popular* **distractors** *– the testing industry's term for "wrong answers," but*
> *ones that will distract the less-prepared -- and way too advanced for entry-level. You are*
> *more likely to have a personal encounter with a living American president than with these*
> *terms during the course of a lengthy real estate career.*

> *Additional "distractor" terms related to classes and characteristics of property include*
> - ***tangible (or corporeal)*** *property, which means **physically touchable, material** property,*
>   *most notably **land and its improvements**, and*
> - ***intangible, (or incorporeal)*** *property, which means such abstract, "untouchable," yet*
>   *very real elements as **mortgages, rights,** and **other encumbrances**, as well as assets*
>   *such as **bank accounts and most financial instruments, like stocks and retirement**
>   *accounts.*

> *Though these terms* **occasionally** *appear in prelicensing curriculum outlines and textbooks, do*
> *NOT expect to be tested on definitions or examples of tangible, intangible, corporeal, and*
> *incorporeal property, since these terms, though they provide useful distinctions, are more*
> *legally refined than is appropriate for an entry-level exam.*

I-B. Land Characteristics and Legal Descriptions   (Expect 2-3 questions from this area)

Land includes the ***earth's surface, subsurface to the center of the earth, the space overhead, and the rights to each***. Some broad categories identifying the most ***common rights in land*** include ***surface rights***, ***subsurface rights***, ***mineral rights***, ***water rights***, and ***air rights***.

> An owner is entitled to handle each of these rights separately and may, for example, lease out
> the right to farm the land, drill for oil, or erect a billboard to three different tenants.

> Three commonly recognized ***physical characteristics of land*** are its ***immobility***, ***permanence*** (or
> ***indestructibility***), and ***uniqueness***.

*All three of these characteristics can be illustrated by the simple example of a **global positioning system (GPS)** reading at a particular spot: **the latitude and longitude reading for that spot cannot be moved, destroyed, or duplicated.***

Four commonly recognized **economic characteristics of land**, or factors that bear on a property's particular value, are **scarcity**, **improvements**, **permanence of investment**, and **area preference**.

*The fact that land is permanent and unique does not mean the land itself is desirable, or that there aren't similar properties available if it is. So, the elements identified above as **economic characteristics** are what add up to making a particular property valuable.*

Property descriptions may be **legal descriptions**, such as **metes and bounds**, **lot and block**, or in certain regions of the country, **rectangular survey**, or less formal, such as a **street address**.

*In some areas, street addresses will suffice to identify properties on listing agreements, but a **full legal description**, meaning one that would not only keep one property from being confused with another but could be precisely traced by a surveyor, **is required for a deed to be valid**.*

Metes and bounds is the widely used system of property description that "walks" the property boundaries by first identifying a physical **point of beginning (POB)** and then describing the distance and directions along the property line, generally, but not always, following a clockwise direction back to the point of beginning.

*A **monument** is any of a number of landmarks that provides a stable point of reference for surveys. They can be natural, such as trees, rivers, or "the northwest corner of the pasture lot near the house in which I live" (from an 1881 New England deed), or artificial, such as **surveyors' stakes**, metal markers, or **"pins,"** stone boundary markers (a.k.a. **merestones**), or a government **benchmark** (see below).*

*With advances in technology, **GPS coordinate readings** of latitude and longitude are appearing more frequently in surveys—and deeds—to fix the location of monuments and other points where the boundary line changes direction.*

Lot and block, or **lot, block, and tract**, system of property description is generally used for **subdivisions**. Also known as the **recorded plat system**, it identifies properties according to a **plat map**, or sometimes even an **assessor's map**, of the subdivision, which in turn shows the specific dimensions of each lot, the access roads, and easements. (**Assessor's maps** almost always have a disclaimer statement that they are "**for tax purposes only**.")

Government rectangular survey, *or* **rectangular survey**, *or even* **rectangular**, *property descriptions are used in over thirty states, mostly in the Midwest and the West. It is a grid system that starts measuring from the axis where a **baseline**, an east-west line, and a **principal meridian**, or north-south line, intersect.*

*Six-mile by six-mile squares are known as **townships** and are identified by where the **township line** (east-west) and **range line** (north-south) are in relation to the principal meridian and* *baseline. Each township contains 36 one-mile squares, or **sections**, each of which in turn is ordered and numbered. Four townships add up to a **quadrant**.*

*Property descriptions using this method are commonly presented in terms like, **the SW 1/4 of the SW 1/4 of Section 22, Township 15 South, Range 13 East, Gila and Salt River Base and Meridian, Arizona**.*

*Since the rectangular system is **NOT** in national use, many state licensing agencies prohibit testing on this method within the general portion of the exam used in their state.*

This method is definitely NOT used in all of PSI's client states, which makes it a 'nice to know' not a 'need to know' topic for licensing tests in those states, especially since it does nothing more to help protect the in-state public for licensees to know details of this method than their knowing the capital city of Canada; it should NOT be on the test.

*Some of the above terms in boldface **MAY**, however, appear on tests as distractors, or be tested as part of the state-specific portion of the exam in states where applicable.*

Vertical land descriptions are necessary for defining air rights, as in specifying the floor-to-ceiling sale of ***air lots*** in multistory condominiums or cooperatives (which are generally governed by state-specific ***horizontal property acts***), as well as subsurface rights for mining and drilling. Terms related to vertical descriptions include

- ***geodetic survey system*** refers to the U. S. Coast and Geodetic Survey System, which established a series of markers nationwide that serve as permanent reference points for orienting accurate surveys
  - ***benchmarks***, the name for these permanent markers, are typically brass disks set in concrete and/or stone that identify the latitude, longitude, and elevation of the marker
- ***datum***, which is a term for the point, line, or surface from which elevations are measured; there are local and national datum for reference in establishing local and national benchmarks for surveys

Physical descriptions of property and improvements will include questions that may actually be introduced and discussed in other areas but are written to provide scenarios and applications of those principles, especially as they apply to definitions of lots and property particulars used in listing or previewing property for a client.

For example, a question might focus on the description or size of a particular lot, or other site or construction considerations, such as lot size, structure dimensions and square footage, and livable area. The following should be useful in understanding these basics:

A ***lot,*** or ***site***, is the parcel of land under consideration. ***Lot size*** is an important element in a property listing, and can either be determined ***by computing the area defined by the legal description in the property's deed*** or ***by reviewing the*** taxing authority's ***assessor's data***, which often gives the lot size in acres; assessor's data is typically found in a printout known by such names as a ***field card***.

Neither of these methods is foolproof, and depending on the particular property, it may be prudent, even necessary, at some point in the transaction to have the boundaries and lot size *confirmed through a professional property **survey**, which will determine **the accurate location and dimensions of property boundary lines** as well as identify encroachments.*

*It is worth noting that while acreage is a unit of area commonly computed according to the **conventional acre**, also known as a **survey acre**, which is **43,560 square feet**, in some areas, assessors—and builders—may use an **assessor's acre, which is 40,000 square feet**.*

One way to picture the assessor's acre is by imagining a 200' x 200' square parcel, which is very easily subdivided mathematically, especially when compared to the 208' 8-1/2⁺" x 208' 8-1/2⁺" square parcel that makes up the conventional acre's additional square footage.

So be cautious when using acreage data, and remember this distinction if you find conflicting data once you are a practicing licensee—it may be the reason for the difference.

For test purposes, the survey acre of 43,560 square feet will be the standard size, unless specifically noted as otherwise.

Historical note: *For centuries, English-style metes and bounds measurements were made in units known as **links** (7.92"); **rods, or poles, (16.5' [25 links]); chains (66' [4 rods; 100 links]** or **66'); furlongs (660' [10 chains; 40 rods or poles]); and miles (5,280' [8 furlongs]).*

*Stories of the original American surveys make reference to these terms, particularly to **Gunter's chain**, which had 100 of the 7.92" links to make up its **66'**; it is also worth noting that the still-common **mile (5,280')** was tied directly to the now-obscure furlong long before being legally defined as 8 furlongs by an English Act of Parliament in 1593, after which it became known as the **statute mile**, and later, in the United States, as the **survey mile**.*

*(For those of you who love a little Latin, **mile** comes from the Roman army's measurements of **a thousand paces**, "**mille passus/passuum**," where a **pace** equaled **two steps**. While this originally came to about 4,850' (1,618 yards), it has since been legally standardized in America and Great Britain as 5,280' (1,760 yards). For those of you who couldn't care less about such things – oops! Five wasted lines of reading!)*

*Interestingly, **furlongs** as a measurement linger on . . . some cities, such as Chicago and Phoenix, have eight blocks per mile, which means each one is a furlong, or 1/8 of a mile (5,280' divided by 8 = 660'). Also, furlongs are used in horseracing: the Kentucky Derby is run at Churchill Downs racetrack, which is 10 furlongs, or 1.25 miles long. And **a surveyor's acre is** defined as 10 square chains, which is the same as **a furlong in length by a chain in width**, giving us **660' x 66' = 43,560 square feet**. So these old measurements are still with us!*

Test note: *Although most of the units above are historical terms now widely considered obscure, some surface occasionally in modern real estate practice, so may appear on a stray exam question asking about terms related to old metes and bounds descriptions.*

Important property-specific details for listing and marketing property include determining the ***physical dimensions*** of the primary structure and any outbuildings along with the ***basic type of construction*** for each, such as masonry/stucco, brick, or framed with siding.

Further, a physical property description should identify *utilities, such as availability and hookups, type of heating and cooling*, whether there is *private or public access to water and sewer*, and if the property is in compliance with building codes that govern its construction and occupancy.

In the course of gathering data from the public records regarding a subject property, a licensee should research the *tax assessor's records*. These will generally identify the property acreage along with the physical dimensions, square footage, and construction type of any buildings on the property, as well as *the zoning code* for the property.

Finally, in *determining the square footage* of a building, the conventional standard among appraisers, and most municipal assessors, is to *use the exterior dimensions* of each floor, even though more and more appraisers also include interior living space dimensions using laser rulers.

So, read test questions carefully to determine whether or not a situation is asking for floor space for, say, carpeting or tile, or gross square footage. If the latter, a structure that is 20' x 40' has 800 square feet. Period.

If the question concentrates on how many feet of floor tile to order, it should include information on how thick the walls are after insulation and drywall, whether there is a chimney-foundation, or anything else that reduces the actual pedestrian-area of the interior space.

*However, for **condominiums, co-ops,** and other units, including PUDs, that are not conventional stand-alone single family residences or commercial buildings, you need to determine **gross living area (GLA)**, which is often measured using interior dimensions, or **"paint to paint,"** of above-grade, finished areas. Also, **areas designated as basements or utility rooms <u>may</u> be excluded from GLA totals**, even if they are considered separately for valuation determinations.*

The zoning code will identify such basic property-use classification, such as whether the property is residential, commercial, or industrial, the minimum lot size required for new construction, and other basic usage restrictions and minimum setbacks from the lot lines for the placement of building construction and other improvements.

*In one municipality, for example, a lot that is zoned **R-40**, or **"one-acre zoning,"** is classified as **"Low Density Residential,"** and requires a minimum of 40,000 square feet in order to build a residence, which cannot occupy more than 35% of the property's total lot size.*

Zoning codes, classifications, and requirements, despite many basic similarities, can vary widely from one municipality to another, and are tied to each one's planning documents.

I-C. Encumbrances and Effects on Property Ownership
(Expect 1-3 questions from this area)

Encumbrances are non-ownership interests, *monetary* and *non-monetary*, that represent *a restriction on the use and/or transfer of real property*.

Three broad types of encumbrances are *liens, easements,* and *encroachments.*

A *lien* is a *monetary encumbrance* that asserts the *lienholder* has a creditor's claim to a specific monetary interest in the property's value. A lien may be satisfied by the property owner through simply paying the debt directly or by paying the debt out of the proceeds of a property sale.

Liens can be categorized as *voluntary*, which means the debt was approved by and acceptable to the owner, such as a mortgage, or *involuntary*, which means they have been placed against the owner's will, such as a tax lien, judgment, or other claims against a property for equity interest.

Voluntary and involuntary liens may be further classified as *general*, which *affects all of a debtor's property and assets*, as in a bankruptcy proceeding or IRS tax lien, or *specific*, (or *special*), which means it *is limited to a specified item controlled by the debtor*, such as a mortgage on a house or loan on a car.

*You may also see references to **statutory liens**, which are created automatically by statute, as with tax liens, and **equitable liens**, which are created by a court order, as in a judgment lien. These are too specialized for test use except as distractors.*

A short list of common types of liens and their broad categories includes
- *mortgage liens*, which result from property financing, are *voluntary, specific* liens
- *mechanic's liens*, which result from non-payment of claims by those who worked on a property, are *involuntary, specific* liens
  - *materialman's liens*, a category of mechanic's lien, which may result from non-payment of claims by those who provided materials for a property, are *involuntary, specific* liens
- *special assessment liens*, when they result *from an owner's request* for the improvement, are *voluntary, specific* liens
  - *special assessment liens*, when they result *from a municipality-initiated improvement*, are *involuntary, specific* liens
- *municipal property tax liens*, which result from unpaid taxes, are *involuntary, specific* liens
- *federal (IRS) tax liens*, which result from unpaid taxes, are *involuntary, general* liens
- *judgment liens*, which result from a court order to pay a certain amount to a creditor, are *involuntary, general* liens

Liens are generally effective the day they are *recorded*, or officially filed, in the appropriate office of public records.

*In some states, like Connecticut, this means town or city hall, depending on the municipality, since **not every state observes a county system for recording land records**. Exam questions **may** refer to <u>counties</u>: Oops! Think **town or city** instead.*

In the event more than one lien is recorded, the *priority of liens* for payment after a voluntary or forced property sale typically goes by *date of recordation* from the first to the most recent. However, the government is a line-jumper, and *property tax liens are always superior to other liens*, regardless of when they became effective.

*Note: **mechanic/materialman's liens follow state-specific rules** for time limits on recording the lien, such as within one year of the project, as well as determination of the lien's effective date. **Commonly**, though, **they are effective as of the date work***

began, *not the date of recording, and represent an enforceable lien for a statutory period after recording, generally a year, unless satisfied or renewed.*

Non-monetary encumbrances include such physical and legal restrictions as **easements** and **encroachments**, both of which may restrict the use and/or transfer of property. *They also include* **subdivision covenants, conditions, and restrictions (CC&Rs)**, *and* **owners' association rules**, *most commonly* **homeowners' association (HOA)** *rules, for most common-interest ownership arrangements; these will be mentioned again in Topic Area II-D, Private Controls.*

Easements are interests in land that give a nonowner the right to use a property for a specific purpose, generally to cross over it. Easements affording access are commonly distinguished as either **appurtenant** or **in gross**.

An **easement appurtenant**, or **appurtenant easement**, is the right to use one property for the benefit of another one. The most common example is a **right-of-way** across someone else's land to get to one that has no other access. The rights to enter, exit, and reenter are sometimes referred to as **ingress**, **egress**, and **regress**, respectively.

An **easement by necessity**, or **easement of necessity**, is a special, but common, type of appurtenant easement that arises automatically in cases where an owner sells a **landlocked parcel** of a larger property.

In these situations, the property that provides, and must allow, the access is referred to as the **servient tenement**, or **servient estate**, since that property is a 'servant' to the interest of the one that requires it. The land that 'commands' the benefits of this use is referred to as the **dominant tenement**, or **dominant estate**.

Appurtenant rights and interests such as those above are said to **run with the land**, which means they typically remain in full force even if omitted from the language of a deed during a property transfer.

Future sales of properties with an easement appurtenant should include clear reference to the easement in all applicable documents to not only clarify the scope and limits of the easement, but to help assert and ensure its continued existence.

An **easement in gross** differs from an easement appurtenant in that **there is only a servient tenement**. For example, a **utilities easement**, or **utilities pass-through**, for sewer pipes and telephone lines do not benefit a utility company's physical property, so there is no neighboring dominant tenement, but **the servient tenement owner must allow access for maintenance and repairs**.

Other common examples of **easements in gross** are **those for personal use**, as when an owner lets a neighbor or friend cross a property as a shortcut or to get to a waterway. Such **personal-use easements** are typically not transferable, and terminate with the death of either party or the sale of the property.

However, owners that allow others to use their land without a specific arrangement may lose the right to stop that use if it becomes protected by law through an *easement by prescription*, or *prescriptive easement*.

Prescriptive easements must meet several legal tests, most notably, that the use of the property has occurred regularly for the minimum *statutory period* required by state law.

This period of *adverse use*, meaning that *the use may have adverse consequences on the owner's unencumbered property rights*, may be fewer than ten years or longer than twenty, depending on the state. *Questions about years will be on the State exam!*

Other conditions for acquiring an easement by prescription include several particulars about *the pattern of use*. Typically, the use must be characterized as *open*, *notorious*, and *hostile* in the legal meaning of these terms.

Similar terms arise in different real estate textbook and legal dictionary definitions of prescriptive easements. The following terms may be understood as incorporated into the legal meaning of their closest match above: visible, continuous, exclusive, and adverse.

Also, such property use is more likely to entitle the user to an easement by prescription if the owner is unaware through years of neglect than if the owner has knowingly allowed the use to occur.

Some legal authorities recommend posting a sign indicating "Private Property: Use by Permission" or "Walkers Welcome" on a subject property to thwart prescriptive claims by providing open, public notice of permissive use.

Consult a lawyer regarding these matters: a landowner may need to record a notice of 'interruption of use' within the statutory period to ensure that the owner's rights are legally protected. Also note that new neighbors may be entitled to go back to claim the time of a previous owners' use through tacking.

According to <u>Black's Law Dictionary</u> (10th ed., 2014), tacking may allow an owner to meet the statutory requirement quite quickly by "the adding of one's own period of land possession to that of a prior possessor to establish continuous adverse possession for the statutory period."

This all means that simply changing ownership of either the potential servient or dominant tenement does not necessarily reset the statutory clock.

Complicated stuff, since a current owner's legal entitlement to tack on prior periods would almost surely require a judge's ruling and depend on clearly demonstrating a relay-race style of the same "open, notorious, and hostile" use by current and immediate past owners.

For **test purposes**, *just remember that **tacking** is the principle by which **a new owner may be able to claim a previous owner's period of similar adverse use to satisfy a statutory minimum-period requirement.***

Though this term is unlikely to appear on a test, except as a distractor, it is a good example of how seemingly simple terms could suddenly open a world of complications in specific real estate transactions.

It also illustrates how learning about such wrinkles might not only be professionally valuable by helping clients anticipate and address property problems (or opportunities!), but have direct application for yourself as a property owner to either protect your property or ensure a continued use.

In some more public cases, such as when a private entity owns a road or gathering place used by the public, that entity may publish a notice and/or block off the private property one day a year to formally assert its continued right to do so. (See also **property dedication** in Topic Area VIII-D.)

Prescriptive easements are often confused with "adverse possession," a second type of **adverse use**; it is **a form of involuntary alienation. With adverse possession of a property, actual title is transferred** based on demonstrated use similar to that needed for a prescriptive easement's right to continue a specific use.

Party wall easements are just what the name suggests: a common building wall or a stand-alone wall either on or at a property line, and therefore involves both owners in ownership, maintenance, and/or access issues.

Creation and termination of easements represents a longer, more detailed list than is worth itemizing here, given their relatively self-evident nature, legal technicalities, and low importance for entry-level testing. However, a few of the most common categories include
- **creation of easements** may arise through
  - **mutual agreement** of the parties, either in writing (**express**) or through behavior (**implied**)
  - **necessity**, as with certain landlocked properties
  - **longtime use**, as in a prescriptive easement
- **termination of easements** may occur through
  - **abandonment** of use
  - **release of easement** by the owner of the dominant estate
  - **conclusion of the reason** for the easement
  - **merger of the dominant and servient estates** through purchase of one property by the owner of the other

A **license** is a personal, revocable right or privilege granted by an owner to someone else to use the property, typically in a brief, limited way. **A license**, which is often simply a verbal approval, **can be seen as changing a trespasser into a visitor**. It is **not considered a type of easement** and may or may not include compensation. Examples include tickets to use a parking lot, attend an event, or watch a movie in a theater.

Encroachments are a special type of encumbrance that involve *some form of overlapping use of one property by another*, as when a portion of a building actually crosses the line, known technically as *trespass*, or tree limbs or a roofline extend across a property boundary, known technically as *nuisance*.

Whether or not such close calls as those above are encroachments are often resolved by either a *visual inspection* or a *property survey*, which determines *the accurate location and dimensions of property boundary lines*. Surveys are also used to *discover unrecognized encroachments*.

Encroachments are legally categorized as *unauthorized and/or illegal infringements that can affect a title's marketability*, but they may arise and exist with the knowledge and consent of the owners.

An encroachment *may affect the marketability of title for both properties* unless it is adequately addressed. Depending on the situation, some simple encroachments may be removed by
- *selling the property* in question to the encroaching property owner
- *deeding the use as an easement*

Another property encumbrance that affects the marketability of a property's title is a *lis pendens*, which is Latin for "*pending lawsuit*."
- If a *lis pendens* has been recorded against a property, it means that *some form of litigation against the property is pending* that *may become the responsibility of a new owner* to address.
  - *This term also appears in upcoming Topic Areas as a defect in title or a title insurance issue; it may be categorized and tallied for testing in those areas if the question relates more to a title defect or title insurance than a type of recorded property encumbrance.*

I-D. Types of Ownership   (Expect 1-3 questions from this area)

Title refers to both the *ownership* of something as well as to the *legal evidence of ownership*, such as a *deed*.

The degree and type of ownership gives rise to a variety of *types of title*, such as the following ones that are often mentioned in the marketing and transfer of ownership
- *clear title*, or *good title*, which refers to a title *free of restrictions that would limit its transfer*
- *marketable title*, which refers to a title that *a reasonable buyer would accept as a clear title*
- *equitable title*, which refers to *the holder's right to acquire ownership and formal legal title*, as when a *prospective buyer has entered into a valid, enforceable contract* to purchase a property; *this title interest may be sold, assigned, or transferred by the prospective buyer*
- *legal title*, or *bare legal title*, or *naked title*, refers to the holder having *apparent ownership but not full title*, as when a seller has entered into a binding sales contract, thereby

relinquishing equitable rights to the buyer, or when a lender requires the right to hold legal title during the loan period

> **NOTE:** *The last two types of title, **legal** and **equitable**, represent the primary pair regarding basic legal rights of lenders and borrowers. Though too legally involved for entry level testing, **legal theories about who holds and controls <u>legal title</u> and subsequent rights are at the heart of mortgage lending and foreclosure laws nationwide** and will be described briefly in Topic Area IV-D, Mortgages/Deeds of Trust.*

> *You may also encounter the term **color of title**, which is defined as anything that **appears to give title**, but does not—the proverbial deed to the Brooklyn Bridge is an obvious example. Also known as **apparent title**, the appearance can be fostered by forged, inaccurate, or outdated deeds, or other legally insufficient ownership/transfer documents regardless of whether the holder knows about or is unaware of the flaw.*

> ***Color of title** and **apparent title** are too legally refined for any licensee to "need to know," but **could easily appear as distractors**.*

<u>Forms of ownership: Ways to "take title," or "hold title"</u>

Sole ownership, or ***tenancy in severalty***, or simply ***severalty***, means that an individual is the sole owner of a property.

Concurrent ownership, or ***co-ownership***, refers to ownership by two or more parties at the same time. Among the types of concurrent ownership are

- ***tenancy in common***, under which the parties, or ***tenants in common***, hold an ***undivided fractional interest in the property***. For example, three family members may own a house together as equal one-third owners, or two may own 25% each and the third owns the remaining 50%. In either case, the fractional interest does not convey either the use or ownership of separate thirds, quarters, or halves of the house itself or other physical property to any of them. *Also, **each tenant may hold a deed that does not name any of the other owners**; compare with **unity of title** below.*
- ***joint tenancy***, under which the parties, or ***joint tenants***, hold an ***undivided*** rather than uneven shares. The following considerations apply to this form of ownership
  - the ***four unities***, which refers to the following ***set of legal requirements for creating a joint tenancy***
    - ***unity of title***, which means all parties are ***named on the same deed***
    - ***unity of time***, which means all parties ***took title at the same time***
    - ***unity of possession***, which means all parties have ***undivided possession and use rights***
    - ***unity of interest***, which means all parties have an ***equal interest***
      - *this is a basic concept and **general questions will assume interests must be equal** despite at least one state, Connecticut, allowing unequal interests, but **for general questions, think equal; Alaska has gone even further by abolishing joint tenancy altogether as a method of property conveyance**, following the lead of Ohio and Oregon; **such state-specific amendments <u>may</u> appear on that portion of the exam***

- the *right of survivorship**, meaning that as each individual joint tenant passes away, the remaining tenants' interest would increase until **the last remaining person becomes the sole owner**; this condition is **historically an assumed part** of a joint tenancy, and **some older deeds will specify "as joint tenants and not as tenants in common"**

  > ***state laws and court rulings** in some states have interpreted **some joint tenancy arrangements** as being **the same as a tenancy in common**, and do not consider the right of survivorship as automatic

- *joint tenancy with right of survivorship*, under which the objection noted immediately above is removed **by specifically including "with right of survivorship"** in the language of the deed; *sometimes seen abbreviated on forms and financial instruments as **JTWROS** or **JTRS***

  - *Non-testable note*: some textbooks illustrate this concept by referring to joint tenancy ownership of any asset as *"a poor man's (or person's) will,"* since ownership automatically transfers from a deceased owner to the remaining one(s) by operation of law without requiring either a written will or probate approval; a properly drafted legal notice should be recorded, though, to ensure clear title for the survivor(s)

- *marital property ownership rights*, which **do not exist in over a dozen states** and **vary from state to state where they do**, include

  - *tenancy by the entireties*, or *tenancy by the entirety*, which has the same unities as a joint tenancy, but adds the concept that the couple owns the property as one indivisible legal unit, which provides broad property protection against creditors; it exists in some form in over twenty states, including our Western neighbor, New York

  - *community property*, which is generally understood to mean that property acquired by married people during the marriage is owned by both, unless it is exempted by one party acquiring it as separate property through gift, inheritance, or separate funds; there are nine community property states

    - *AZ, CA, ID, LA, NV, NM, TX, and WA are the eight "traditional" states; WI recognizes community property rights by a state Uniform Marital Property Act*

  - *community property with right of survivorship*, which strengthens the estate transfer and tax benefits of the survivorship right of the remaining spouse, has become applicable in most of the above nine states within the past ten years

Common interest ownership is a type of ownership that refers to multiple owners having an overlapping, inseparable interest in a property complex; **condominiums**, **townhouses**, **coops**, and **timeshares** are the most common examples and will be discussed below.

Condominium ownership grants the owner (1) *fee simple title to the unit* <u>and</u> *(2) an undivided interest in the jointly owned common areas as tenants in common* with the other association members.

The **condominium** form of community ownership also has several components that go by various similar names, depending on the state. In general, though, condominiums are created through some form of state-approved **horizontal property act** that allows ownership of the unit's airspace.

Condominium status is achieved when a developer's organizational plans, widely known as the **declaration**, are recorded. The declaration typically includes a copy of the **bylaws**, **legal** *descriptions and surveys*, which identifies common areas as well as units, and a list of *restrictive covenants*, also known as the *covenants, conditions, and restrictions (CC&Rs)*.

In addition, the developer typically creates a *condominium owners' association* for the self-governing of the property by the unit owners. This association is responsible for ongoing upkeep and maintenance of common areas, which it funds by assessing and collecting each unit's proportionate share of cost through *association fees*.

> The municipal tax authority taxes the unit owner directly for the assessed value of the unit. Like an owner of a detached residence, *the unit owner is directly and solely responsible for taxes*: the association has no liability for unpaid unit taxes.

A *townhouse*, or *townhome*, or *row home*, is one of a row of homes sharing a *common wall*, or party wall, *with a neighbor on either side (except for end units)* and *no units above or below*. Although there may be common elements, such as a central courtyard, *townhouses differ from condominiums in that there is actual ownership of land from the ground up, sometimes with a small private yard*. Typically they are constructed with multiple stories; three-story townhouses are often called "trinities."

Cooperative ownership, or a *co-op*, or *coop*, looks similar to a condominium to the general public, but the unit occupant does not own the unit like the condo owner does. Instead, the occupant is a *shareholder* who owns *stock* in the company that owns the complex, and in exchange for agreeing to *obey the bylaws* and *pay the co-op's fee*, generally billed monthly, is granted a *proprietary lease* interest to occupy the specific unit.

> Put simply, *the unit "owner" owns stock, not real estate*; the stock entitles the stockholder to a *leasehold interest* in a specific unit's possession and use.

> Unlike the condominium form of ownership, the *cooperative corporation is liable for the entire building's property taxes* and *collects them from the owners through the co-op fees* that are prorated for each unit's proportionate size and value within the complex. These *prorated fees* are also the way the corporation collects other operating expenses and assessments.

Timeshare ownership is typically characterized by *fee simple ownership* of *interval occupancy of a specified unit*, although it may take the legal form of a right-to-use contract that simply conveys *a contractual fixed-year, recurring-use* of a specific unit.

> Either way, the unit, generally an apartment unit at a resort property, is *available to the owner for the specified period every year*, such as the first week of June. *It may also involve being able to "bank" the week* and exchange it for a *"floating use"* week at a different participating timeshare site.

Planned Unit Developments (PUDs) represent another type of common interest ownership that is important to municipal plans and may earn a test question.

PUDs are a specialized category of subdivision that is ***both a regulatory process and a type of building development***. A ***PUD encourages mixed land use***, and may include clustered residential properties with open space, recreational, commercial, and even industrial areas.

> *PUDs often allow developers to integrate multiple land uses with a more flexible application of zoning restrictions, such as smaller residential lots and reduced setbacks, to meet overall community zoning goals. Not unlike condominium ownership, units are individually owned in fee while common areas are either owned and managed jointly or deeded to the local government and reserved for PUD-resident common use.*

Corporate and business ownership structures *are generally more intricate than those sketched above; they will be touched on briefly in Topic Area XI-B, Commercial, Industrial, and Income Property.*

As noted above, in its broadest sense, ***estate*** simply means everything one owns, ***including both real and personal property***.

Estates in real property can be either ***freehold estates***, which means owned property, or ***nonfreehold estates***, also known as ***leasehold estates***, which means leased property.

> *Leasehold estates, including why they are classified as **personal property**, will be covered in Topic Area VII-F, which concentrate on leases, leasehold estates, and property management topics.*

The ***bundle of rights***, or ***bundle of legal rights***, *is a common illustration of property ownership that compares the entire set of ownership rights to a bundle of sticks. (The bundle contains private rights; the government reserves additional rights to itself.)*

> *Each stick represents a separate, distinct ownership right, such as the right to possess and use it, exclude others from it, and rent, sell, or mortgage it.*

> *As any stick is given over to someone else, the absolute and complete ownership is increasingly limited by those who now control a "stick."*

Freehold estates commonly imply ***fee simple***, or ***absolute and complete ownership of real property***; in other words, they often come with ***the whole bundle of rights***. The key distinctions for testing are that a freehold estate may or may not include conditions on its use and/or transfer.

> If there are ***no conditions on its use and/or transfer***, it may be known by any of these interchangeable terms: ***fee, fee simple, fee simple absolute***, or ***estate in fee simple***.

> *Note: This is one of the first of many cases to come in this book in which* <u>Black's Law Dictionary</u> *confirms that different terms are synonymous. As noted in the Introduction, the purpose of "extra" terms where applicable throughout this book is to show you some of the alternate ways "your" term may appear on the test.*

If there are conditions on its use and/or transfer, there are some common conditions that may take a variety of forms with long, elegant, impressive, and often interchangeable names. Those most commonly mentioned in textbooks and used for ***distractors on tests*** include

- ***fee simple defeasible***, or ***defeasible fee***, or ***qualified fee***, which means that the deed or title has some sort of qualification of its use that makes it subject to being annulled or voided and reverting to the original owner or some third party. Two types include
  - ***fee simple determinable***, also known as ***qualified fee***, or ***determinable fee***, which means that should a stated condition occur, the estate automatically ends and grantor has a ***possibility of reverter***, or a ***reversionary interest*** in or ***reversionary right*** to the property.

    For example, someone may deed a property to a religious organization with the condition that if the organization no longer uses the property as intended, the deed reverts back to the grantor, or to the grantor's heirs or assigns as ***reversioners***.
  - ***fee simple subject to a condition subsequent***, *which means that should a stated condition occur, the grantor, heirs, or assigns must take action to exercise a right to terminate the estate under the **power of termination**, or **right of entry**, or **right of reentry**. If no one exercises this right, the estate remains under the control of the grantee.*

Phew! How about that "fee simple subject to a condition subsequent"! Think you'll get a question trying to find out if you know how it differs from "fee simple determinable"?

Relax – if you do, shame on the test!

Information like that above is presented throughout this book primarily to expose you briefly to terms and concepts in the very content area where they might appropriately be used as distractors.

Remember, some hard-looking choices taken from the same Topic Area as the correct answer will distract less confident test-takers, who will think, "I knew I should have studied harder – I'll bet the one I don't know is a slightly better answer than the one I think is right."

Bingo! They take the bait! But by seeing it here, <u>you</u> will avoid waffling and recognize it for what it is: a term you've seen, are not afraid of, and know enough about to find when you need it, probably a long time after you've been selling property.

The terms above also demonstrate how quickly a subject area that will only get at most three questions on the actual test can look like a mini-course in legal minutia.

This area, and a few others to come, has enough terms and complexity to give rise to some delightful charts in real estate textbooks, as well as earnest contention among their authors about which of several interchangeable terms is the more correct.

In fairness to the more advanced and/or obscure material presented both in textbooks and here, it is part of the professional language you are learning to speak, so you should be no stranger to it.

Remember, though, that while this is an important area to understand in general, this Topic Area, like most others, will only contribute a few questions to the test.

And those questions on the test are MOST likely to be testing the more common and important topics, not the obscure, 'weird,' or 'tricky' ones.

So relax: you're not studying for the legal bar exam. Plus, you get to miss a few and still pass. Now, back to the "real" subject . . .

A *life estate* is another category of estates in property, one that conveys an estate for the duration of the life of the *life tenant*. For example, a parent may deed the family home to an heir but retain the right to use the property for life. Or a husband may will his wife a life estate in a house they share for the duration of her life with it going to his children from a previous marriage upon her death. *Unless specifically restricted, a life tenant may move out and use the property as a rental for life.*

Other situations include such circumstances as a university buying—or being "gifted"—a house adjacent to campus under the condition of allowing a life estate use for the sellers. So, life goes on as usual for the occupants, often plus extra cash from the transaction, and the university eventually gets possession and full control.

There are a few related terms for life estates, including
- *conventional life estates*, which arise by intentional arrangements among the interested parties, as in the situation above
  - *life estate pur autre vie, which means a life estate "for the life of another" in French, measures its duration by the life of someone other than the life tenant, as when a caregiver or companion is allowed to live in a property until the death of the specified other person*
- *future interests*, which refer to the right to acquire the estate upon its termination as a life estate. They typically take one of the following two forms
  - *remainder*, or *remainder interest*, which means the grantor of the life estate has named someone else to take title; such an individual is referred to as a *remainderman; this would be the case in the situation above about a parent leaving a spouse a life estate—the heir(s) would be remainderman/remaindermen*
  - *reversion*, or *reversionary interest*, which means the estate reverts to, or is returned to, the grantor of the life estate, who is known as a *reversioner; this would be the case in the situation above about a university purchasing a property and granting a life estate*
- *dower* and *curtesy*, which are once-common terms now used in fewer and fewer states to refer to the property inheritance rights of widows and widowers, respectively; some state have statutes that address rights of a surviving spouse

*Note: as noted above about other terms, entry-level licensees do not <u>need</u> to know about "**life estate pur autre vie**" arrangements at time of licensure -- these estates are rare enough that many seasoned brokers—and many lawyers—may never have encountered one.*

*Plus, an attorney would draft any such estate document. So, while the term is common textbook fare, it is rarely, if ever, tested. It is, however, like the terms **dower** and **curtesy**, a favorite term for use as a distractor.*

While you should have a general familiarity with all of the terms above, the more intimate details and nuances of all of these types of estates, as well as those of the upcoming section, exceed the professional expectations of real estate licensees and are properly left to real estate attorneys.

*In fact, to offer opinions or interpretations, or to prepare documents, on these matters could subject you to a suit for **practicing law without a license**. **Always tell clients to get a legal opinion on legal details from a practicing attorney**.*

- ***This point will be further emphasized—and tested**—in Sections related to Agency Relationships, Responsibilities, and Ethics in business practices; see Topic Areas V-A, V-C, and IX-F, respectively.*

But knowing more than you need to pass the test can be a handy thing for later on: a listing licensee in South Carolina was recently sued by a would-have-been buyer for not having discovered that the "seller" only had a life estate interest in the property.

Speaking of specific states, there are two Louisiana-unique encumbrances of general interest here that are definitely off-limits for testing, except, perhaps, in Louisiana

- ***usufruct** refers to a Louisiana-only term for a type of estate similar to a life estate, though it may be for a less-than-life period; a usufruct grants the right to use a property, including renting it out and keeping the rent monies*
  - *the **usufructuary** is the owner of the usufruct*
  - *the **naked owner** is the one who actually owns the property and has what is referred to as **naked ownership**; a **naked owner** is similar to a **remainderman** (or sometimes a reversioner) in a life estate.*
- *Louisiana also recognizes a **right of habitation**, which is when a person has not been granted a full usufruct but does receive **a nontransferable real right to dwell in the house of another**.*

This ends the presentation of key terms and concepts likely to be either tested or used as distractors in this Content Outline Section.

II-A. Government Rights in Land (Expect 1-2 questions from this area)

The *four government powers* are *police power, taxation, eminent domain*, and *escheat.*

Police power refers to the State's authority to provide for the general welfare of the community through legislation and a range of *enabling acts*, or *enabling statutes*, that authorize agencies to organize and both implement and enforce their obligations.

Zoning, which will be covered in more detail in the next Topic Area, is a primary mechanism for municipalities to implement their police power by establishing regulations controlling how land is used.

Taxation is a government power necessary to raise revenue for municipal expenses, like schools and roads; the governmental right to set taxes allows a municipality to assess properties, levy taxes, and sell the property if the taxes go unpaid.

Typically, real property is assigned an **assessed value** by the municipal government's assessor's office that is then used as the basis for annual taxation for **general assessments**, which raise funds for the entire municipality.

These **general real estate taxes** are also called **ad valorem** taxes, which means they are taxed **"at value,"** so that properties with a higher assessed value pay proportionately more than those with a lesser value.

Practical note: assessed values for tax purposes rarely match, or even intend to match, a property's actual, current, fair market value, although the two are commonly confused by the general public. One reason for this is that the assessment values may remain unchanged for years, whereas current market values are subject to constant change.

A property may also be subject to **special assessment** taxes if there are certain improvements, such as neighborhood sidewalk construction or streetlight installation, that benefit the immediate area only.

The governmental **power of taxation includes the power to place liens** on property in the event of an outstanding special assessment or unpaid general taxes. These include **special assessment liens**, **municipal property tax liens**, and **federal (IRS) tax liens**, all of which were previously listed as types of encumbrances in Topic Area I-C, Encumbrances.

Note: taxation issues span multiple content outline Topic Areas, including details regarding tax liens in Topic Area I-C, Encumbrances; and both details and calculations of tax math in Topic Area X-C, Property Tax Calculations.

Eminent domain is another government power. It refers to the **taking** of title to real property for some use, public or private, that has been judged by the appropriately authorized governmental entity to be beneficial to the community's interest, as with certain utility or industrial expansions. It is most commonly exercised, though, for civic improvements such as road or school construction projects.

Eminent domain represents a type of ***involuntary alienation of property*** and involves (1) the process of ***condemnation*** and (2) ***payment of just compensation*** to the displaced owner.

Eminent domain proceedings generally begin with an attempt to negotiate the purchase of the subject property, which, ***if the owner rejects the offer***, typically leads to the government or authorized entity to ***file a notice of condemnation in the land records***.

This action sets the stage for ***court hearings*** on the matter during which the owner gets to respond to the attempt to take the property. ***If the government prevails, proceedings are held to establish a fair market value for the property***, which can be accepted or disputed by the property owner. Ultimately, the owner gets money and the government takes title.

*Eminent domain is a power granted by the Fifth Amendment to the Constitution of the United States (1791) in what is referred to as **the "takings clause"**: **"nor shall private property be taken for public use, without just compensation."***

In practice, the determination of what constitutes "just compensation" is subject to court battles, and is rarely as simple as it looks.

Also, condemnation under eminent domain is entirely different from the condemnation of property under safety or health codes.

*In **Kelo v. City of New London (2005), the U. S. Supreme Court** affirmed that eminent domain can be exercised for a municipality's economic benefit even in cases where the transfer is from private residential owners to private business owners. In this case, Susette Kelo's "little pink house" was among those that, despite a fight against being "taken," were ultimately bulldozed for corporate and business projects promised by private developers in the Fort Trumbull neighborhood, a longstanding residential area adjacent to Fort Trumbull, a pre-Civil War fort with Revolutionary War origins and a highly desirable river view.*

This controversial decision resulted in state-level protections nationwide against businesses attempting to use eminent domain to acquire property based on arguing that their ownership would provide higher tax revenue and other economic benefits, such as new jobs and increased local commerce. In New London, even more than ten years after the Supreme Court decision, most of the flattened Fort Trumbull area remains undeveloped, and untaxed!

Escheat is also one of the four government powers. It refers to the transfer of property ownership from an individual to the State when the individual dies ***intestate***, or without a will, and ***with no known heirs***. The transfer is often phrased as ***reverting*** to the State.

Escheat also transfers certain types of property to the State at the end of a statutory period of inactivity, as with dormant bank accounts or abandoned property.

Property, such as land or bank accounts, that escheats to the State may be available to be claimed by heirs or owners once they make their interest in the property known.

Most states hold such property as custodians under a state-specific Unclaimed Property Act, and have an "unclaimed property" area on their Website to help owners or their heirs reclaim abandoned property – have a look!

II-B. Public Controls Based in Police Power   (Expect 1-2 questions from this area)

Zoning is a type of *police power* under which municipalities can regulate land use. This begins with a *master plan*, or *comprehensive plan*, or *general plan*, that identifies the broad economic objectives and goals and seeks to achieve them through classifying certain areas or buildings as usable for specific purposes, such as residential, retail, industrial, and agricultural.

Nonconforming use in zoning refers to a property *continuing a prior use after a zoning change*. For example, a commercial area that has been rezoned residential may include a building that has a corner grocery. It may continue to sell groceries, though if it closes, it may have to be converted into residential space.

A common residential example of nonconforming use would be *an existing house on a small lot in a neighborhood that has been rezoned* to require at least one acre for new construction. The house will generally be *"grandfathered"* and allowed to remain on its now "substandard" lot; typically it can be rebuilt if destroyed. *Rebuilding or home improvement plans are generally prohibited from expanding "the footprint"* of the grandfathered structure's existing foundation or assessor's external dimensions.

A *variance* also allows for a use other than the primary zoning category, and may be *granted after review by the zoning authorities*. Examples include a restaurant in a residential area or a hairdressing salon in a renovated portion of a family residence.

A *conditional use*, or *special use*, is similar to a variance, but differs primarily in that it is typically more restrictive, and therefore governed by a *permit* that can be revoked if the holder does anything not specifically allowed.

Spot zoning is also similar to a variance, but differs in that the parcel or small *area in question is actually rezoned* to allow it to coexist within an area of different zoning requirements.

Other common zoning terms include
- *setback*, or the specified distance a building must be from a property line
- *buffer zone*, or area that serves to separate one use from another, as when an open stretch is required to separate a new industrial park and an existing school
- *zoning ordinances*, which are simply municipal regulations governing zoning and land-use requirements
  - *building codes*, or *housing codes*, which are governed by zoning ordinances and outline the local requirements for construction standards
  - *building permits* are typically required to begin new construction or significant renovations; they serve to notify the municipality of intended improvements and allow the municipality to review the plans for conformity with codes
  - *certificate of occupancy*, or *CO*, is typically required in order for residents to move into a newly constructed building or return to a renovated one

Special study zones are areas that contain *one or more natural hazard, such as flooding, earthquake, landslide, coastal management, or another geological hazard specific to that area*. These zones can be identified and defined for closer review by any combination of federal, state, and local governments.

Special study zones may have applicability to specific listed properties, and there are a variety of requirements that MAY apply to property sales in special study zones.

For example, both coastal and inland areas nationwide fall within a "Special Flood Hazard Area" according to the Federal Emergency Management Agency (FEMA) Flood Insurance Rate Map that indicate whether special property insurance is required.

And California legislated the Alquist-Priolo Special Studies Zone Act that requires disclosure to homebuyers that a property is in an area with one or more active earthquake faults that may be hazardous to structures.

As part of working for clients, licensees should be familiar enough with their market territory to know if any properties they will be showing—or listing—are within a special study zone.

Also, licensees should ensure that they are aware of whether the property is subject to restrictions due to being in or near a designated wetland area or serving as a habitat for an endangered species.

If so, the licensee should perform the due diligence of identifying the implications of a study zone or other restriction on property ownership, such as whether it requires mandatory flood insurance or zoning approval for property improvements, and then both disclosing and explaining these factors to buyers.

Licensees and owners who demonstrate *willful negligence* in discovering and/or disclosing any of the above environmental problems that might reasonably be associated with a property may be subject to legal action.

These environmental hazards will be repeated, and perhaps tested and tallied, in Topic Areas VI-D/E, Material Facts; they are presented here to illustrate the scope of Police Powers.

The area of *water rights* is one that also demonstrates the exercise by government authorities of police power. These rights are especially full of twists, turns, terms, and statutory controls, so will get some extended attention here. *(The term water rights appears on PSI's Expanded Outline in Topic Area I-B, and may be tallied there for testing, but these rights are more logically discussed in relationship to how these rights are controlled and regulated.)*

Water rights come in many forms, both above and below ground, and may include such terms and concepts as
  • *riparian rights*, which are the rights of an owner to the use of a flowing watercourse, such as a river, pond, or lake that borders the property or a stream that crosses one's land. This term

is generally understood to refer to a ***commercially nonnavigable waterway***, and gives an owner who borders on it ***ownership to its middle***.

- ***littoral rights***, which are those an owner has to the use of frontage on an ocean, sea, or large lake. This term is generally understood to refer to ***commercially navigable waterways***, and gives an owner who borders on it ***ownership to the high-water mark***.

Property may be added or removed by water's action due to floods, droughts, storms, tidal action, currents, sediment deposits, or changes in the course of a river or stream as described by

- ***terms of addition***, such as ***accession, accretion***, ***alluvial***, ***alluvium***, or ***alluvion***, ***reliction***, and ***dereliction***
- ***terms of reduction***, such as ***erosion***, ***avulsion***, or ***deliction***

While the terms above are important to owners, some are about as obscure and special-interest as they come. Nevertheless, it is good to have a basic-recognition awareness of water-related terms, and they may turn up as distractors.

*A water right of great significance in some of the more arid Western and Southwestern states is the **prior-appropriation doctrine**, or **doctrine of prior appropriation**.*

*This doctrine asserts that those along a waterway may take all they want regardless of those downstream. This is commonly summarized as "**first in time, first in right**," and generally assumes that the water will be taken for reasonable and beneficial uses.*

*However, in some states and/or counties where this doctrine prevails, the government may reserve that right and allow others to use **surface water** as well as **groundwater**, or water that is in the ground and tapped by drilling, by **permit**.*

This doctrine and subsequent government control is critical in areas where water is limited yet necessary for irrigation, industry, and/or residential use.

*The opposing doctrine for water use is the **riparian-rights doctrine**, which rules that all owners benefiting from bordering a river or stream have equal rights to use the water passing by or through the property. So, owners upstream cannot deprive those who own property downstream by damming or redirecting the watercourse.*

These doctrines and their local applications may be tested on state-specific portions of those states' state-specific exams; the terms themselves may appear as distractors.

An additional public control based in police power is a ***judgment lien*** on real property, which ***results from a court order*** to pay a certain amount to a creditor; *this term appeared and was defined earlier as a type of encumbrance.*

II-C. Regulation of Environmental Hazards (Expect 1-2 questions from this area)

Environmental regulations, both federal and state, are public controls grounded in the government's ***exercise of police power***.

Each of the following types of hazard has its own set of requirements for acceptable levels as well as ***abatement, mitigation, and cleanup requirements***.

Though a licensee needs to be aware of each hazard and be able to explain its general treatment considerations, certified professionals will generally be required to identify, document, and then address the actual presence of any environmental hazard. This would include determining contamination levels and making legally acceptable decisions regarding how to proceed with any proposed property sale or development.

On the federal level, the ***Environmental Protection Agency (EPA)*** has primary responsibility for most environmental ***regulations*** and ***enforcement*** for environmental Acts such as

- ***Comprehensive Environmental Response, Compensation, and Liability Act (CERCLA)*** (1980), or the ***Superfund Act***, which established prohibitions, requirements, and liabilities concerning closed and abandoned hazardous waste sites, and established a trust fund to provide for cleanup when no responsible party could be identified. It was amended by the
    - ***Superfund Amendments and Reauthorizations Act*** (1986), which, among other things, stressed the importance of permanent remedies and innovative treatment technologies in cleaning up hazardous waste sites, and provided new enforcement authorities and settlement tools
- ***Resource Conservation and Recovery Act (RCRA)***, which is a 1976 amendment to the ***Solid Waste Disposal Act*** and also regulates the hazards involved with municipal and industrial waste generated nationwide
    - the ***Underground Storage Tank (UST)*** program was a 1984 amendment
    - the ***Leaking Underground Storage Tan (LUST) Trust Fund*** for some UST sites was a 1986 amendment
- ***Oil Pollution Act (OPA)***, which is part of the ***Clean Water Act***, and regulates responses and responsibilities for oil contamination

   The particulars of Superfund, RCRA, and OPA are too subject to funding and legislative changes to provide stable testing material, except for distractors, and perhaps a few very broad questions based on the information above.

   *Also, the **National Environmental Policy Act** (1969) requires certain federally funded projects to submit an **Environmental Impact Statement (EIS)**. This is a highly complex document, not entry-level information, so will not get elaboration here.*

   *However, you **MAY** see a question that makes reference to it as a document required for special sales; **any such question is MOST likely to be tallied in Topic Area VI-E, Material Facts**.*

Further, the following ***environmental conditions and hazardous materials are governed by discovery and disclosure requirements***

- ***lead-based paint***, which was banned in 1978, so sales contracts and leases for residential properties built ***prior to 1978***, are, because of the ***Residential Lead-Based Paint Hazard Reduction Act of 1992***, required to include a federally approved ***disclosure notice***
- ***asbestos***, which was widely used for insulation and causes lung problems; ***abatement***, *which means to reduce or end, is a term commonly linked with professional asbestos treatments, and generally takes the form of containment by **encapsulation**, or sealing off, or actual **removal** of materials containing asbestos*

- *radon gas*, which is a colorless, odorless gas that the Surgeon General has warned is the second leading cause of lung cancer, arises from the decay of radioactive minerals in the ground and can collect in a basement or other closed areas
- *toxic mold*, which has become a major health hazard in homes nationwide; it often infests humid wall spaces and generally spreads unseen
- *drinking water problems*, such as finding unacceptable levels of coli form or e-coli bacteria and/or adverse chemicals in tap water; generally this applies to properties with their own deep or shallow well rather than municipal water
- *urea formaldehyde foam insulation (UFFI)*, which was used extensively in the late 1970's for wall insulation, and may continue to exude formaldehyde gas, is an irritant and potential cancer-causing agent; its use was discontinued in 1980, but its presence in a property must be disclosed
- *property environmental problems (external)*, such as the on-site or nearby presence and effects of
  - *contaminated soil and/or groundwater*, from faulty septic systems, landfills, chemical discharges, spills, or toxic disposal
  - *underground storage tanks*, particularly *buried and/or abandoned home heating oil tanks*, which may be deteriorating and/or leaking, and contaminating groundwater supplies
  - *protected species*, such as certain endangered shore birds, fish, or nesting turtles, may present limitations on property development that needs to be discovered prior to finalizing a property transfer
- *additional toxic problems* that could arise in property inspections, but *should not appear on the test*, include
  - *polychlorinated biphenyls (PCBs), which are long-banned, were used as coolants and insulators; they are slow to break down and are known to cause liver damage*
  - *polybrominated diphenyl ethers (PBDEs), which are used in appliances as a flame retardant*

All of the above hazardous situations should be discovered or indicated by a thorough, professional *property inspection*, *which may require additional inspections by a specialist* wherever there are suggestions of problems beyond the standard property inspection.

As noted previously, licensees and owners who demonstrate *willful negligence* in discovering and/or disclosing any of the above environmental problems that might reasonably be associated with a property may be subject to legal action.

II-D. Private Controls   (Expect 1-2 questions from this area)

Private controls on property include *encumbrances*, such as certain types of *liens*, *easements*, and *encroachments*, which were all defined in Topic Area I-C, Encumbrances.

But they also extend to other controls on land use including *private restrictions* such as *subdivision covenants, conditions, and restrictions (CC&Rs)*, and *owners' association rules*. These are *non-monetary encumbrances* that encumber the use and/or transfer of property.

Private restrictions, regardless of their label, generally seek to accomplish similar ends, such as allow or disallow pets in a subdivision or complex, or clarify where to put trash and recyclables. Depending on the property type and local conventions for terminology, they may be referred to as

- *deed restrictions*
- *restrictive covenants*
- *covenants, conditions (or codes), and restrictions (CC&Rs)*
- *condominium owners' association rules* for condominium-specific restrictions
- *homeowners' association (HOA) rules* for subdivision-specific restrictions

Private controls and restrictions are often more restrictive than local zoning ordinances, which means they may either *enhance or detract from property values*, and *in a conflict between CC&Rs and zoning ordinances, generally the more restrictive will prevail*.

Private restrictions on land use are *contractual rather than statutory* and are prepared by *subdivision developers* as well as *individual property owners* to limit the use of a property by future owners. For example, a *developer* may sell lots with restrictions on building styles or property uses, and *property owners* may later decide to restrict the height of shrubs and trees or the colors allowed for exterior house use.

CC&Rs, as well as most other enforceable deed restrictions, *are generally available in the public record*; in the event a resident violates a restriction, another lot owner can seek a *court injunction to stop violators* and enforce compliance.

Note, however, that *illegal restrictions, such as those that violate federal Fair Housing laws, are not enforceable*.

Exam Note: *test questions about non-government property encumbrances that focus on their effect on land use rather than being a type of encumbrance may be tallied in this Topic Area.*

This ends the presentation of key terms and concepts likely to be either tested or used as distractors in this Content Outline Section.

III. Valuation and Market Analysis (8 questions)
(4 Topic Areas; 12 Sub-Topics—each will be covered in its respective Topic Area)

III-A. Value (Expect 1-2 questions from this area)

Value is a broad term for the monetary worth or price of something, or whatever else it might bring in exchange.

There are a variety of *types of value*, including

- *market value*, or *fair market value (FMV)*, which is best understood in real estate to mean *the most probable price a property would bring in a competitive, fair, and open market*, in other words, the *price an informed seller is willing to accept* and *an informed buyer is willing to pay*
- *appraised value* is generally intended to <u>*estimate market value*</u>
- *assessed value*, which means *the value a taxing authority has placed on a property* for purposes of tax computations, and *NOT a current, actual market value*, even if the tax documents assign the label "Fair Market Value" to a property value
- *loan value*, or *mortgage value*, which is the maximum amount a lender will lend
- *insurable value*, which is the maximum amount an insurance company will insure
- *insured value*, or *agreed value*, which is generally the face value of an insurance policy coverage
- *actual cash value*, which is an insurance determination of the *depreciated value* of a property, or *replacement cost minus accrued depreciation (see the end of the next Topic Area for more on the complex appraisal principle of depreciation)*
- *condemnation value*, which identifies what the property is worth to the condemning authority *in an eminent domain proceeding*
- *estate value*, which is the value given on the probated asset list for the real property of a deceased owner; *estate appraisals typically assess the property's value adjusted to match the exact date the owner died, regardless of when the appraisal is performed*

All property values include some commonly understood *elements of value*, which are
- *utility*, which means that it is useful for something
- *scarcity*, which refers to the available supply
- *demand*, which is a combination of *the desire to own it* and *the ability to purchase it*
- *transferability*, which means that *it can be sold or exchanged*

Further, the term *"value"* is *not directly interchangeable* with either *price* or *cost*, since circumstances may create significant differences. For example, the *cost* of a $20,000 addition to a house generally does not add the same amount of resale *value* to the property.

Similarly, the *market price*, which is *the price a property actually sells for*, *may vary considerably from* its *appraised value* or *market value* depending on factors an appraisal or comparable sales do not consider, such as *the motivation of either party to depart from an estimate of fair market value.*

For example, an owner might sell a property for considerably less than market value to a family member, or a buyer may pay more for either sentimental or investment reasons.

General influences on property value include applications of the principles of value identified throughout this Topic Area, often in combination with other considerations, such as *overall market conditions*, especially *market cycles of ups-and-downs*, which take into account *the economic climate and the supply of properties that are in demand.*

However, the real estate adage that *"the three most important considerations in property value are location, location, and location"* leads us to list of some *factors that make location* so important; *location is often considered the single most important element in property value*. The value of a particular location, though, involves national, regional, local, and neighborhood considerations of how the following elements apply to a property:

- *economic trends and circumstances*, which include elements such as
  - local business and employment opportunities
  - labor force composition and diversity
  - availability of private utilities, such as phone service and cable
- *government controls, regulations, and services*, such as
  - taxation
  - zoning restrictions
  - anticipation of the exercise of eminent domain
  - availability of public utilities, e.g., water and sewer
  - schools and other municipal services
- *physical/environmental conditions*, such as
  - annual weather patterns
  - natural resources, such as mountains, lakes, or seashore
  - topographical elements, such as soil types and wetland, swamp, or desert
  - possible hazards, such as hurricanes, flooding, or mudslides
  - recreation areas and outlets
  - local industries and potential air, soil, and water pollution
- *social trends*, such as
  - region and municipality demographic makeup
  - neighborhood cycles and population changes

Property-specific considerations are generally at the center of all value considerations. Some of the property-specific factors to consider may include, but are not limited to

- *overall condition*, such as whether it is new construction or a "handyman special"
  - *property depreciation is a critical term associated with property condition and value, and is discussed in detail as an appraisal principle in the next Topic Area; it is defined as the loss of value resulting from any cause*
- *construction type*, meaning both design style and materials
- *amenities*, which could be *internal*, such as an indoor Jacuzzi, *or external*, such as a better view of some attractive sight than the neighboring properties offer
- *site improvements*, which means *additions to the raw land* such as a residential or commercial building, detached garage and other outbuildings, landscaping, gardens, wells, septic, or connections to public utilities
- *defects*, such as structural problems or negative actions of past owners that have made it a *stigmatized property*, or *psychologically impacted property*

- *historic value*, if any, such as being on the National Register of Historic Properties or being near an historic site
- *aesthetic factors*, such as a unique architectural design, attractive appearance, or "curb appeal"
- *distance from, and access to, population centers, work, shopping, and major roads*
- proximity to *special study zones*, such as *earthquake, flood,* and other *geological or environmental concerns,* such as *wetlands, mudslides, and volcano activity*

*Questions based on **principles of value** are identified by PSI's expanded outline as being tallied in this Topic Area; however, most of the key terms and concepts of appraisal principles are listed as being treated in the next Topic Area. To keep them all together, they are clustered below, so get ready—here they come!*

III-B. Methods of Estimating Value/Appraisal Process
(Expect 3-4 questions from this area)

The most basic definition of an *appraisal* is *an estimate of value*, and it is critical to remember that *appraisals do not <u>determine</u> value, sales do*—appraisals merely estimate property value.

Generally speaking, people commonly "appraise" a property's value while simply driving by, tossing off remarks like, "That place could go for a million bucks, easy."

However, within the real estate profession, a licensee learns how to perform a closer review and prepare a *competitive market analysis (CMA)* based on the professional appraisal methods and principles below; a CMA would provide a more probable estimate of a property's value than the simple drive-by. *Usage note: in some areas or real estate firms, "CMA" is short for "comparative market analysis"—the meanings are synonymous.* (CMAs are the subject of the next Topic Area.)

Except for a very few states, appraisals must be prepared by a licensed appraiser rather than by a real estate licensee. So, the term "appraiser" will be used in this book when referring to appraisals and the appraisal process and "licensee" will be used when referring to the party preparing a CMA or noting other differences between a CMA and an appraisal.

The *purpose of an appraisal* is, in most cases, to provide *an estimate* of a property's specific type of value *as of a specified date*, which may differ from the date of the report, that will in turn *support the use intended by the person who ordered the appraisal*.

Appraisals are commonly used for special purposes, such as defending against a municipal over-assessment for taxes or setting a date-of-death value for estate purposes. So, both the purpose and the effective date vary depending on its intended use.

Since the value of a property can change suddenly and dramatically due to disasters, accidents, or other events, *the appraisal value*, though generally unaffected for some time, *cannot be guaranteed as accurate for any other time than the specified effective date*.

To grasp this concept, simply consider the value of most New Orleans properties the month before and the day after Hurricane Katrina raged through in 2005.

In the course of a full-scope appraisal, an appraiser will analyze a property based on considering each of the following *three approaches to value*, though only one will have primary applicability to determining the final appraisal value of any particular property.

> *The three approaches are (1) the **direct sales comparison (market data) approach**, (2) the **cost approach**, and (3) the **income approach**. Each one will be laid out after the following basic elements of the appraisal process and principles are covered.*

The *appraisal process* can be defined as an *orderly, concise, and systematic procedure for reaching an estimate of value*. It generally follows a common sequence of procedures, which can be summarized by the following check-list

- *define, or state, the problem*, which means clarifying the purpose and scope of the appraisal
- *determine the data needed* and *collect it*
- *determine the highest and best use* of the land and the improvements
- *estimate the property value* using the three approaches to value
- *reconcile the data*, which means to analyze it and settle on a final value estimate
- *prepare the final report* of the value estimate

The *appraisal report* prepared in the final step of the process will follow a format appropriate to the purpose of the report, from a detailed narrative to a simple two-page Uniform Residential Appraisal Report.

Regardless of length, the report will present, analyze, and summarize the data supporting the appraiser's *reconciliation* of data and *final determination-of-value estimate*.

In performing an appraisal, an appraiser will collect and interpret a wide range of data. Some of the common *principles of property value* used by appraisers and real estate licensees alike include the principles of

- *substitution*, which looks at the maximum amount it would *cost to buy an alternate property* that is the same as the subject property, *either by a comparable replacement or an exact reproduction*; this principle is *central to the first two of the three approaches to value* described later in this Topic Area
- *anticipation*, which estimates value based on *looking ahead at the value, positive or negative*, on a property *due to possibility of future changes* to either the property or its surroundings, such as changes in zoning, local economy and businesses, or the character of the neighborhood; this principle is *primarily used in the income approach to value*
  - *plottage*, or *plottage value*, which refers to *combining adjoining properties into a single property* with a total value greater than the sum of their separate plot values due to a more profitable use for the larger property. The *process of assembling* these properties is known as *assemblage*.
- *highest and best use*, which determines *the use that will produce the greatest current value, or the most profitable return on investment*, as exemplified by a developer converting a vacant urban industrial building into profitable residential condo units
- *balance*, which refers to *the mix of land uses that maximizes value* for all of the properties involved, as when the proportion of residential, commercial, recreational, industrial, and other uses make *a general area or building complex* attractive to both residents and businesses

- *supply and demand*, which simply applies this common economic principle to real estate. It can be readily seen by *considering the supply, demand, and cost for an acre of land in central Manhattan versus an acre of land in many Southwestern desert areas.*
- *competition*, which means that *if a particular property is yielding high profits, similar ones are likely to follow* and try to get in on the action
- *conformity*, which means that all *properties in a given area are likely to benefit from being similar to the others*, as in a subdivision of new homes. When conformity is ignored, it can affect property values in either of the following directions
  - *progression*, which is the *benefit a smaller property receives* from being among larger, more valuable ones; *unfortunately, the value increases from progression may backfire on current owners through higher assessments, and taxes!*
  - *regression*, which is the *negative impact on the value of an large and/or expensive property* when it is in an area of smaller, lower-priced, or run-down properties
- *contribution*, or *increasing and diminishing returns*, which makes a cost/benefit analysis of *the actual increase in property value based on the cost of an improvement*, as in how much more a house will sell for after a $7,000 kitchen renovation. If the $7,000 kitchen only adds $2,000 to the property's market value, it would be considered an *overimprovement.*
- *depreciation*, which in an appraisal valuation refers to *the loss of value resulting from any cause*. Two key terms associated with depreciation are
  - *deterioration*, which applies to *physical factors*, such as normal *wear and tear* as well as poor and/or *deferred maintenance or prolonged neglect*
  - *obsolescence*, which applies to *outdated functionality* or *non-property influences*

The *three types of depreciation* used in valuations/appraisals, plus whether or not they are *curable*, meaning they can be remedied, or *incurable*, meaning they are not cost-effective or feasible to fix, are

- *physical deterioration*, which refers to *any downturn from the original condition* of the property, such as an old roof, weathered paint, or broken windows
  - *curable* physical deterioration includes *economically feasible repairs*, such as new exterior paint job
  - *incurable* physical deterioration includes *excessive, cost-prohibitive repairs*, such as correcting a seriously damaged foundation after a landslide or other natural disaster
- *functional obsolescence*, which refers to *outdated design or safety standards*, such as a two-story, three-bedroom house built in the 1920's that still has its original wiring and a single bathroom on the second floor
  - *curable* functional obsolescence would generally include wiring upgrades and new plumbing in the house noted above
  - *incurable* functional obsolescence is generally identified after *weighing the value added* to the property *by the cost of any upgrades and finding the "cure" cost-prohibitive*, sometimes even in comparison to tearing down a property and starting over altogether
- *external obsolescence*, or *economic obsolescence*, or *locational obsolescence*, which refers to *surrounding influences on a subject property*, such as the discovery that a nearby factory has contaminated the groundwater supply, or a pig farm is located just

upwind of the subject property—*style note: for clarity, test questions often refer to this as **external (economic) obsolescence***

- *curable* external obsolescence – **no such thing**, since it arises from factors "external" to the owner's direct control, and someone else must cure it
- *incurable* external obsolescence **is the only kind**, since **spending money on the subject property cannot reverse the actual problem**

For appraisal purposes, **only improvements can be depreciated. Land simply loses value**, and even when it does lose value, as it typically does when the property suffers from external (economic) obsolescence, in the process of determining overall property value, **this loss is categorized separately from the loss of depreciated improvements**.

Estimates of property value, according to appraisal standards, require an analysis of a property based on each of the following **three approaches to value**; as noted previously, only one will have primary applicability to any particular property.

#1: The **first approach**, the **direct sales comparison (market data) approach**, compares the **subject property**, or **subject**, which is the one being appraised, to similar properties, or **comparable properties**, or **comparables**, or "**comps**," **that have recently <u>sold</u>** in the local market, *generally within the past six months to a year.*

> **Style note**: *the above term for this approach is a common testing convention, since it combines the terms **direct sales comparison**, **sales comparison**, and **market data**, all of which represent regional and local usage to identify this actual "sales data" research, compilation, and comparison approach to value. **Be prepared to see any of these synonymous terms used separately on the PSI exam.***

This comparison is used to estimate the subject property's **relative value in the same market** that produced **the sale** of the comparables. This means that **the sale of a comparable must be fair and open** rather than a foreclosure, tax, auction, estate, forced, special-interest, or insider sale.

This approach to value is **an application of the principle of substitution**, since it assumes that similar properties are similarly desirable and may be substituted for each other. This approach is widely and **extensively used for residential properties**.

When available, **three or more comparables are reviewed** and analyzed to provide a balanced estimate.

The **price of a comparable gets adjusted up or down** based on valuable differences between it and the subject property – **the final figure is applied to the subject**.

> For example, if the subject and the comparable houses **were identical except one has an extra bay in its garage**, the value of the extra bay would be used to adjust for price comparisons.
> - **If the comparable has the extra bay**, the value would be **subtracted from the comparable's sales price** to estimate the market value of the subject property.
> - **If the subject property has the bay**, the value would be **added to the comparable's sales price** to estimate the market value of the subject.

All relevant property conditions, including influences from *depreciation*, are factored into the final estimate of value using the direct sales comparison (market data) approach.

The *direct sales comparison (market data) approach* is also commonly, though more loosely, used by appraisal companies in preparing *assessments for municipal taxation*, often referred to as *mass appraisals*, as well as by licensees in preparing a *CMA*. *(As previously noted, see the next Topic Area for more on CMAs.)*

#2: The *second approach*, the *cost approach*, estimates value based on *what it would cost to buy the land and build comparable replacements* for all of the property improvements.

*This approach was once also known as the **summation approach**, since it "summed-up" the value of the land and all individual improvements on it. This term, though obsolete, may appear on your test—it is simply an old synonym for the cost approach.*

The *cost approach is also based on the principle of substitution*, since it assumes that no rational person will pay more for a property than the amount it would cost to purchase a comparable site and construct a comparable building without any undue delays.

The cost approach is commonly *used for commercial properties, as well as for special-use properties* that do not have many comparables, such as *churches, schools, and municipal buildings*.

In order to adjust for the difference between new construction and existing improvements, the *current structures are evaluated for depreciation, which is then subtracted from the new construction cost*.

There are *five steps* in the preparation of a cost approach analysis. These are
1. *estimate the value of the land only*, as if vacant
2. *estimate the new construction cost* of all improvements
3. *determine the accrued, or combined, depreciation* from the three types of depreciation (see the end of this Topic Area) as they affect the current improvements
4. *subtract the accrued depreciation* of the improvements from the estimate of new construction to get the estimated value of the current improvements
5. *add the value of the land to the value of the improvements*

The completion of the last step will produce the *estimated property value by the cost approach*; *because the cost approach "sums-up" individual elements, it is occasionally referred to as the summation approach, so watch for that on the test!*

There are *two methods for determining the new construction costs* of improvements needed for the steps above: *replacement cost* and *reproduction cost*.
- *Replacement cost* determines *the current cost of an acceptably similar copy*, often somewhat more contemporary in functionality and construction.
- *Reproduction cost* determines *the current cost of an exact copy* of the improvements, flaws and all, such as outdated features or construction materials of older buildings; *this is often seen in estimating costs for recreating historical buildings or building similar properties for aesthetic purposes.*

There are several ways to estimate the above construction costs, including the **square-foot method**, the **unit-in-place method**, the **quantity survey method**, and the **index method**. *Details of these appraisal methods are best left to appraiser exams.*

However, the **square-foot method** is so commonly used in practice for estimating a wide variety of new-construction that it may appear in math questions.

To compute construction costs using the square-foot method, simply **multiply the cost-per-square-foot of building a comparable property by the square footage of a new building**.

So, if a 10,000 square foot warehouse were built for $397,500, or $39.75/square foot, a 12,000 square foot warehouse would cost $477,000.

#3: The **third approach**, the **income approach**, estimates the present value of future net income of income-producing properties through the process of **capitalization**, which converts **future income projections into current value**.

The **income approach** is **based on the principle of anticipation**, which asserts that value is created by the expectation of benefits to be derived from **return on investment** during ownership as well as any capital gain realized at resale.

The **capitalization rate**, or **cap rate**, is the term for the **rate of return** on the cost of the investment.

To **compute the capitalization rate** for a particular property, simply **divide the property's net operating income by its price**.
- For example, a $200,000 property that has a $20,000/year net operating income has a capitalization rate of 10 percent.

The following **three categories of income** are important to remember for rentals and other investment properties. *(All of these will be repeated and used in Topic Area XI-B, Commercial, Industrial, and Income Property.)* **The last of these is the one to use for computing cap rates.**
- **potential gross income**, or **projected gross income**, or **scheduled gross income**, which means the **maximum rental income** at 100 percent occupancy
- **effective gross income**, which means the **actual income** after subtracting vacancies and rent collection losses
- **net operating income (NOI)**, which is **what's left of the effective gross income after subtracting all of the property's operating expenses**, such as maintenance, taxes, insurance, reserves for replacements, and other recurring expenses (but not debt service, such as mortgage interest)

To **estimate a property value from a cap rate**, an appraiser, licensee, or investor may analyze several recent comparable sales to determine their cap rates, develop an appropriate composite cap rate for the subject property, then **divide the subject property's NOI by the cap rate**.
- For example, if the appraiser determines that a cap rate of 5 percent is what the area market is currently supporting, and the NOI for a property is $10,000, the estimated property value would be $200,000.

Another income approach method of estimating value is the *gross rent multiplier (GRM)*, or *gross income multiplier (GIM)* method. This is a simple, informal rule-of-thumb technique that is often used for one-to-four unit residential rentals or small commercial and industrial sites.

Using recent sales, the appraiser *divides each comparable property's sales price by its gross income, either monthly or annual*, using the same time-period standard for all, to determine their respective GRMs.

Then, after developing a representative GRM from a reconciliation of the collective GRMs, the appraiser *multiplies the subject property's income by the GRM* to arrive at a general estimate of value.

- For example, if the appraiser develops a GRM of 135 for monthly rents in an area, and is analyzing a property with a monthly rent of $1,200, the property's value would be expected to be around $162,000.

In practice, the income approach is very sensitive to property differences and complexities, highly specialized analysis techniques, and disagreements among appraisers about applications.

The above explanation of the income approach is intentionally very basic, and is presented more to expose you to a few terms you may see on the test than to provide a short-course in this appraisal method.

III-C. Competitive/Comparative Market Analysis (CMA)
(Expect 1-2 questions from this area)

The above broad definition of an appraisal does not adequately distinguish between an *appraisal* performed by a professional appraiser and a real estate licensee's *competitive (or comparative) market analysis (CMA)*.

The following additional description helps define the role of an appraiser's appraisal in property valuation compared to a CMA

- *an appraiser's* appraisal is performed by a licensed appraiser or, in some states, a state-approved real estate licensee, and is a *more extensive analysis* than a CMA because it *follows a set of comprehensive guidelines* outlined in the *Uniform Standards of Professional Appraisal Practice (USPAP)* and results in one of several standard-format *appraisal reports*
- a formal appraisal report, rather than a CMA, is typically *required by lenders or insurers* to support *a property value that has been more rigorously researched in support of the accuracy and legal accountability of the actual risk they are assuming*

So, the role of an appraiser in property valuation is to prepare a *formal appraisal*, which provides *stronger documentation* in support of its estimate of value for use by others, such as lenders, insurers, and tax assessors.

Nevertheless, the less rigorously researched licensee's *CMA* is still useful for estimating property value, typically using *three or more comps that have sold within the past year. Though a CMA is not as "official" as an appraisal and is generally compiled using "rule of thumb" approximations rather than precisely researched data, if carefully prepared, it will often result in a final figure that is roughly the same as that of a formal appraisal.*

A broker's price opinion (BPO) or broker's opinion of value (BOV) are terms used in some areas for what are sometimes an even more informal valuation than a CMA. Often no more than an oral "educated guesstimate" or a one-paragraph letter in response to a 'general value' inquiry from a financial institution or curious individual, they are often subject to both state regulations and company policies.

> *In one state, for example, it is legally prohibited to accept compensation for a BPO <u>unless</u> the BPO is intended to result in a listing, and even then, the fee must be credited back as an advance on earned commission if the listing leads to a closing.*

A licensee's CMA is typically used to establish a **reasonable listing price** for sellers and a **reasonable offering price** for buyers.

Despite the figures in a licensee's CMA estimate, **it is the seller's responsibility to set a list price** and **the buyer's responsibility to determine an offering price.**

A licensee's role in preparing a CMA involves **gathering, interpreting, and computing the value of comparable properties** as well as performing other **property-related math**. Therefore, some of the appraisal topics raised above may be directly applicable within this Topic Area, including non-math questions about preparing a CMA for income properties by using comparable Gross Rent Multipliers or Gross Income Multipliers.

> However, if a question involves a computation instead of an interpretation, it will most likely be tallied in the Topic Area X-E, Calculations for Valuation.

> *This area will include **appraisal-type questions**, but **from the perspective of a licensee who is preparing a CMA**; watch for the use of "licensee," "broker," or "agent" rather than "appraiser" in CMA questions.*

> *The emphasis in this area may include scenario-type questions that have examples of **how a licensee reviews a property for age, condition, and defects**, and then **discusses and/or explains** these factors and their effect on the property's value with the owner or prospective buyer.*

Some of the property conditions that might be used in these examples include
- **general property information** for the listing, such as age, condition, or zoning
- **material defects**, which are defects that would affect a potential buyer's decision on either buying the property or how much to pay
- **internal environmental problems**, such as the existence of lead paint, asbestos, radon, or toxic mold
- **external environmental problems**, such as contamination or pollution
- **stigmatizing conditions**, or **psychologically impacted properties**, such as a history of illegal activity, death, suicide, or health information about either a seller or past residents
- **adjustments to comparable properties**, such as extra amenities and features that make the subject property different from particular comps
- **depreciation considerations** as they apply to the subject property's final value

III-D. Appraisal Practice; Situations Requiring Appraisal by a Certified Appraiser

(Expect 0-1 question from this area)

Widespread, often fraudulent, overvaluation of real estate led to bank failures nationwide in the mid-to-late 1980s.

In response, the federal government mandated the establishment of professional standards and licensing for appraisers, and required lenders making ***federally backed residential loans*** to support their values ***with an appraisal by a certified appraiser***.

> *The Appraisal Foundation was established in 1987 by Congress to foster professionalism through establishing generally accepted professional valuation standards and licensing qualifications, the former through the Appraisal Standards Board (ASB) and the latter through the Appraiser Qualifications Board (AQB).*

> *Under AQB guidelines there are two broad categories of appraisers: **certified general appraisers**, who are qualified to appraise all types of real estate, and **certified residential appraisers**, who are qualified to appraise all residential real estate.*

> *Every state has its own licensing requirements for appraisers, and generally implement AQB's guidelines for classroom education, field experience, and examinations for each category of appraiser.*

Though lenders and insurers may require a formal appraisal on any property, it may be a ***company policy rather than a legal requirement*** <u>***unless***</u> ***government funding is involved***.

> *Ever since the last half of 2007, the residential real estate market, the financing industry, and the stock market have been hit hard by widespread defaults and foreclosures stemming from subprime borrowers failing to keep up with their mortgage payments, notably those that were structured as Adjustable Rate Mortgages (ARMs) and had reached a scheduled rate increase (see Topic Areas IV-A and IV-B in the upcoming Outline Area for more).*

> *Since much of this has been attributed to lenders accepting a combination of "optimistic" appraisal figures, often ones that anticipated property appreciation, and a similarly optimistic assessment of a borrower's ability to pay, expect to see more changes in both government regulations and lender requirements for conservative appraisals. (Also watch for more stringent requirements, including licensing, for mortgage lenders and brokers.)*

> *Questions on this situation, as important as it is, are unlikely to appear on your test. However, if you are familiar with the trend to hold appraisal professionals accountable for appraisals that are neither tailored to nor influenced by lender or borrower objectives, you should be able to answer any that might pop up.*

<u>This ends the presentation of key terms and concepts likely to be either tested or used as distractors in this Content Outline Section.</u>

IV-A. General Concepts

(Expect 1-2 questions from this area)

There is an extensive list of terms for *general concepts* related to financing, since *financing instruments can be intricately tailored to the particular situation*, and involve a lot of time-honored as well as new and creative concepts.

Some of the more common terms in property financing include
- an *instrument*, which is a written legal document or contract defining rights, duties, and other obligations
  - a *secured instrument* is one that has some form of *collateral* identified as *alternate compensation* in the event the borrower *defaults*, or fails to perform, according to the instrument, or contract.
- *equity*, which refers to *the amount of principal, or after-debt money, a property owner has in the property*; for example, if a property worth $250,000 has a $200,000 loan balance against it, the owner has $50,000 of property equity
- *liquidity,* which refers to an asset's being readily convertible to cash; *real estate is generally not considered a highly liquid asset, at least at fair market pricing, since it takes time to market property and close on a sale*
- *points* refer to a measurement unit for loan costs -- *one point* equals *one percent of the face value of the loan*
- *yield* is the term for the *return* or *profit* a lender makes on a transaction, *generally expressed as a percentage of the amount invested*
- *loan-to-value ratio (LTV, or L/V)* is a ratio *obtained by dividing the loan amount by the property value*, which is taken from *the lesser of the appraised value or the sales price*. For example, a loan of $80,000 on a property valued at $100,000 has an LTV of 80 percent. Clearly, *the lower the LTV, the lower the risk of loss for the lender* in the event a borrower defaults and the lender has to sell the property.
- *leverage*, which refers to *the amount of money borrowed in relation to the property's value –* high leverage, or a *high LTV*, equates to a *large loan amount* coupled with a *low downpayment*
- *private mortgage insurance (PMI)* typically refers to *policies that cover the "top" portion of the loan amount, generally no more than 30 percent*, against early default, since the property's value might not cover the entire remaining loan balance due after other foreclosure costs. Lenders making *high LTV conventional loans* commonly require the borrower to protect the lender against default by purchasing PMI, which *thereby lowers a lender's risk and sometimes allows them to lend upwards of 95 percent LTV.*
- *buy-downs* refer to an *up-front sum paid by a borrower specifically to reduce the interest rate and thereby bring down the monthly payment*. The reduced rate may be temporary or permanent, depending on the arrangement.
- *lock-in commitment* is *a lender's charge* that prospective borrowers may elect to pay in exchange for the lender's promise to fund the loan at a quoted interest rate even if the lender's rates change before the loan is funded at closing
- *annual percentage rate (APR)* is the term for the *effective* annual percentage rate, or *true annual cost of borrowing*; it allows more accurate consumer comparisons of lenders and financing offers by taking into account all loan charges and fees, such as points and prepaid interest, rather than just identifying the interest rate applied to the loan balance.

- *APR details are defined and regulated by the **Truth in Landing Act (Regulation Z)** – see Topic Areas IV-E and IX-C for more on TILA and Regulation Z.*
- *conforming loans* refer to loans that ***conform to a set of lending specifications, especially standard maximum limits on property values*** or requirements for borrower credit worthiness
  - *nonconforming loans* typically involve greater risk on the part of the lender by relaxing the standards for property values, LTV, and/or borrower credit history
- *prime interest rate, prime rate,* or often simply *prime*, refers to ***the rate charged by banks to their most creditworthy customers***, generally large corporations, and are generally the same or very close to those of other banks; the Wall Street Journal defines it as "The base rate on corporate loans posted by at least 75% of the nation's 30 largest banks." ***It also commonly refers to the rate the Federal Reserve System charges for its loans to banks.*** Prime rates do not adjust at any regular interval.
- *prime* may ***also refer to borrowers*** considered to be of high quality, meaning low risk of default; prime borrowers are typically offered attractively low interest rates
- *subprime* or *non-prime* refers to the ***credit status of borrowers*** with poor, limited, or no credit history, and are therefore unable to qualify for a conventional or conforming mortgage due to the greater risk of default; ***credit scores generally range between 300 and 900, and many lenders consider scores lower than 660, 620, or 600, depending on the lender, as subprime***
- *usury* refers to ***a lender's charging an illegally high rate of interest***. Usury laws vary from state to state, and do not apply at all in some states.
  - *The term originally applied to charging **any** interest on loans and is still **commonly defined as charging exorbitantly high interest**; in legal terms it refers to charging a rate in excess of legal limits. **Though your state may not have a usury law (many do not, and thereby serve as "home-base" for credit card companies), this financially relevant concept is still valid for testing**.*
- *predatory lending* is a term closely associated with usury, though it refers to a wide array of practices by which borrowers are taken unfair advantage of, such as extremely severe penalty fees and interest rate hikes after a late payment
  - *This term is finding widespread use in reference to the problems within the mortgage industry based on subprime borrowers' inability to make continued payments and then lose and/or owe money after a property foreclosure sale; many of these foreclosures are triggered by an adjustable interest rate adjusting upward at the end of an introductory period.*

Lenders may also require some of the following additional charges and conditions as part of the processing and funding of certain loans

- *discount points*, often simply called *points*, are ***a lender's up-front charge*** for making a loan; ***points are typically charged to increase the lender's yield when funding a loan at below-market interest rates***; as noted above, one point equals ***one percent of the loan***
- *origination fee* is a lender's ***charge for preparing and processing a loan***
- *document preparation*, or *"doc prep,"* is a lender's ***charge for preparing and copying loan-related documents***
- *funding fee* is also a lender's processing charge, most commonly associated with VA loans
- *impound*, or *reserve account*, which is an ***account for the funds held by the lender to pay recurring expenses, such as property taxes and insurance, during the life of the loan***; known in some areas as an ***escrow account***

- *satisfaction of mortgage certificate*, or, for deeds of trust, a *release deed*, or *deed of release*, required of the seller's lender(s) to confirm that funds have been applied to pay off the seller's loans
- *estoppel certificates*, or confirmation notices from interested parties, such as getting a lender's signature attesting to the exact remaining principal balance or a tenant's signature attesting to the amount of security deposit held by the seller

General *IRS tax issues* regarding the costs, benefits, and tax implications of property financing include the following borrower-related items

- *interest payments* on mortgage loans *are deductible* if the homeowner itemizes deductions, though *for homeowners with low-balance loans and few other deductions, the standard deduction may be better than itemizing*; in practice this is best addressed by tax professionals
- *real estate taxes* are deductible
- *certain costs* of financing and refinancing may be deductible, such as *origination fees*, *discount points*, and loan *prepayment penalties*

The process of reviewing an applicant for a loan typically includes the following components and considerations

- *prequalification* generally refers to a lender, or even a licensee, determining the probable maximum loan amount the borrower can repay by collecting preliminary information about the borrower's financial circumstances, generally during a brief interview. It is a nonbinding preliminary assessment.
  - *The terms prequalified or preapproved are sometimes applied to a fully qualified buyer who is looking for property, as in, "My client has been prequalified by a lender for the amount of financing given in this offer."*
- *qualification* refers to the process a lender goes through of more closely reviewing a buyer's credit and financial status to determine the actual maximum loan amount the lender would fund.
  - This process often includes calculating *debt-to-income (DTI) ratios*, or simply *debt ratios*, which refer to the percentages of a borrower's gross (pre-tax) income that will be allocated to monthly debt obligations; there are *two main kinds of DTI—they will be detailed in Topic Area X-D, since they involve calculations*
  Once approved for funding, the applicant becomes known as a *qualified buyer*, or *approved buyer*
- *credit report* from a major credit reporting agency will be requested by the lender to determine the official status of an applicant's financial history in order to qualify or approve the buyer

When a prospective buyer, qualified or not, finds a property and approaches the lender for funding, *the lender will perform a property review prior to fully approving the loan*. The process of reviewing a property for a loan typically includes the following components and considerations

- *property appraisal,* or *Certificate of Reasonable Value (CRV)* for VA funding, for a current estimate of value
- *title search* or *attorney's opinion of title*, to confirm that the title is unencumbered
- *title insurance policy*, to transfer the risk of loss in the event of undiscovered flaws in the chain of title

IV. Financing

(5 Topic Areas; 26 Sub-Topics—each will be covered in its respective Topic Area)

- *property survey*, if there are any questions about the exact boundaries and possible encroachments or physical encumbrances
- *zoning* codes and ordinances that govern the use and future of the property

IV-B. Types of Loans and Sources of Loan Money (Expect 1-3 questions from this area)

There are a host of ordinary, special, and creative financing options in lending. For the sake of broad categorizations here, *loan types can be distinguished by three primary elements*: *repayment options*, *interest rates,* and *loan purpose*. Clearly, all three categories are present in every loan, but one tends to be more evident in the loan's name.

> Note: The term *"mortgage"* may be substituted for *"loan"* as soon as it is clear that *the loan is, or will be, secured by real property*. *However, "loan" is used here as the default term to keep the primary focus on the basic financing arrangements. The test questions may use the terms interchangeably as appropriate to the topic being tested.*

Types of loans with names that suggest their *repayment options* include
- *amortized loans*, which are those that are paid off over time, usually through equal monthly payments for a set number of years
  - *fully amortized loans*, or *level-payment loans*, are structured to pay down the *loan amount*, or *principal*, plus interest, in *equal payments*, generally paid monthly until the balance is zero. These loans begin with a higher portion of each installment going toward the interest, and end with most of the loan payment being applied directly to the remaining principal.
  - *partially amortized loans* can be structured any number of ways, but typically mean that the principal is paid down according to an agreed-upon schedule, with a final payment that is larger than the others
    - *balloon payment* is the term applied to this sort of large final payment
- *growing equity mortgages* have payments that increase over time with the additional amount applied directly to principal, which brings down the interest payments and overall repayment period of the loan
- *graduated payment loans* are fixed-rate, scheduled payment loans that allow the borrower to make lower payments initially, and increase them to make up for the difference. Similar to growing equity mortgages, they both are structured in anticipation of the borrower's income rising along with the payments due.
- *term loans*, or *straight loans*, or *straight note*, or *interest-only loans*, look similar to a partially amortized loan in that they have single, level payments for the life of the loan with a much larger final payment. However, under a term loan, the *payments are interest-only*, and *the entire principal amount is due* at the end of the loan's *term*, or time period for the borrower to use the capital.
  - since there is no reduction in principal, these are classified as *nonamortized loans*

Types of loans with names that identify their *interest rate structure* include
- *fixed rate loans*, which have *an interest rate that remains the same for the life of the loan*
- *adjustable-rate mortgages (ARMs)*, which have a fluctuating interest rate that gets adjusted at periodic intervals. They typically allow a borrower to pay a *lower rate for the first few years*, which keeps their initial expenses low, then *adjusts either to a preset*

interest rate or a rate based on market conditions at a scheduled, contract-based adjustment interval.

- *interest-only*, which is essentially the more currently used name for many term loans, and *may be structured to allow lenders to adjust the interest rates periodically* according to preset conditions, such as changes in prime interest rates; *these loans require a balloon payment of the entire principal at a contractually set date*

- *variable rate mortgages (VRMs)*, which allow the rate to vary over the life of the loan, generally based on an appropriate index; they are often structured to adjust at six-month intervals with a ½ percent per year cap on increases, and a 2-1/2 percent increase cap over the life of the loan

- *renegotiated, or renegotiable, rate mortgages (RRMs)*, which are loans in which the interest rate is adjusted periodically, general every three to five years, to remain in line with current market rates. *This is a popular financing instrument in Canada, where the Canadian Rollover mortgage is structured to include renegotiated rates every five years.*

Types of loans with names that suggest their *loan purpose or primary characteristic* include

- *construction loans*, or *interim loans*, are loans that are generally paid to the borrower in installments during the course of a construction project. They typically require the borrower to make interest-only payments and arrange for *permanent financing*, called an *end loan*, or *take-out loan*, of some sort at the end of the construction period

- *blanket loans* 'cover' more than one lot, parcel, or property; they are common in subdivision developments, and typically include a *partial release clause*, which allows the borrower to *pay off and release separate parcels* as they get sold

- *package loans* include *funding to purchase personal as well as real property*, as in the sale of a furnished condo

- *wraparound loans* allow a borrower to take out *a second loan*, make a payment *large enough to cover both loans* to the new lender, and have *the new lender make the payments on the original loan*

- *closed-end mortgages* do not permit additional borrowing or prepayment, which allows lenders to offer lower interest rates since the borrower will pay interest for the full term

- *open-end loans* offer a line of credit secured by a property, and are usually created for improvements that will be done in stages, so the borrower's monthly indebtedness keeps pace with actual outlays

- *home equity loans* or *home equity lines of credit (HELOC)* are typically made on an agreed amount of a homeowner's equity in the property, either in a lump sum or a line of credit. They are often referred to as *second mortgages*, or *junior mortgages*, and typically have a lien priority below any other existing mortgages.

- *reverse mortgages*, or *reverse annuity mortgages (RAMs)*, provide payments from a bank to the homeowner, who generally has already paid off any original loans. This is an increasingly popular form of financing among retirement-aged homeowners who want to have access to their equity and leave repayment to their estate or heirs.

- *bridge loans*, or *swing loans*, both often referred to as *gap financing*, are short-term loans made to cover a temporary shortfall or period prior to the funding of the permanent loan

- *nonrecourse loans* are secured loans that allow the lender to attach only the collateral, leaving all other borrower assets judgment-proof in the event of borrower default

- *conventional loans* and *insured loans* are very broad categories that generally refer to *basic loans between an individual and a lender* and *loans that are made with government backing after satisfying certain specific government guidelines*, respectively; *these will be treated in greater detail in the next two Topic Areas*

- *seller-financing* is a type of loan that provides funding for a buyer, and property-secured income for the seller. *(There is more on seller-financing, especially **contract for deed (land contract)**, in Topic Area IV-C, Sources of Loan Money, and IV-D, Mortgages/Deeds of Trust.)*

- *sale/leaseback* financing is a method used by some businesses ***to free up equity*** in a business property by ***selling it to an investor who in turn leases it back*** to the business

- *subprime mortgages **refer to mortgage loans arranged for subprime borrowers**, also known as **non-conforming loans** since they have no set guidelines; due to strong growth in subprime mortgage lending over the past five-to-ten years and subsequent, recent high default and foreclosure rates, you will undoubtedly become very familiar with this category of loans, lenders, and borrowers once you are licensed*

  - ***the subprime lending crisis** has been fueled by abuse of underwriting standards, mostly by mortgage brokers and lenders either inflating a borrower's actual income or falsifying income entirely to make a borrower look capable of making mortgage payments that are, in fact, too high*

Financing sources for buyers who either cannot or simply prefer not to pay cash include ***lending institutions**, **the seller***, and, of course, family, friends, and personal contacts.

In most cases, though, buyers will make arrangements with ***a local bank*** for property financing. ***The local bank or financial institution that originates the loan*** represents what is known as the ***primary mortgage market***, or ***primary market***.

Sometimes buyers are introduced to a lender by a ***mortgage broker***, who operates as a middleman between the public and lenders. Mortgage brokers assess the individual's credit worthiness and then try to match that party with a suitable lender, which could be a local bank, or it could be an institution or investment group in some other part of the country that do not deal directly with the public.

In turn, the local bank, or other lending source, will simultaneously be making, or ***originating***, loans to other buyers, and eventually have a collection, or ***portfolio***, of loans, which it ***warehouses***, or holds, until they can be packaged and sold as a group.

These loans, as a group, may look attractive to a larger financial institution as a ***secured investment***. Once a loan is sold as part of a package like this, it has been ***securitized*** as component of a ***mortgage-backed security***, and enters into what is known as the ***secondary mortgage market***, or ***secondary market***.

If the bank sells its portfolio of loans to a financial investor, the bank regains its capital while shifting the ownership, and risk of default, to the institution in the secondary market. The local bank now has the funds available to make new loans, create a new portfolio, and sell it off. And so the cycle goes.

*The widespread infusion of subprime loans into the secondary mortgage market has resulted in widely publicized financial disasters, largely since investors were not aware of the actual risk of some of these securitized mortgages or the dazzlingly confusing array of **derivative products** tied to **toxic assets**, such as **subprime-mortgage-backed securities**.*

As noted earlier, these problems are affecting the real estate industry by, at a minimum, tightening access to mortgage money and instigating more stringent requirements, including licensing, for mortgage lenders and brokers. During your real estate career, you will certainly have Continuing Education courses aplenty on the ever-churning complexities of this mess.

Conventional financing is one of the three most common financing methods available to **institutional lenders.** The other two are made through the **Federal Housing Administration (FHA)**, and the **Department of Veterans Affairs (VA)**, both of which are discussed more fully in the next Topic Area, IV-C, Government Programs.

Conventional loans are loans made by lending institutions without following any particular government program's requirements. ***These loans typically charge somewhat higher interest rates and require a greater down payment than FHA or VA loans***.

Seller financing may take the form of a **purchase-money mortgage**, or seller **carryback**, in which the seller generally provides **a supplementary loan** to the buyer that makes up the difference between the purchase price and the total of the buyer's other loans and cash.

Or, ***it may take the form of primary financing*** under a **contract for deed (land contract)**, which is a type of two-party mortgage between the seller and the buyer and is discussed in greater detail in Topic Area IV-D, Mortgages/Deeds of Trust.

Seller financing is **attractive in situations where lenders are reluctant to lend**, such as on raw land, or when the seller wants to **'play bank' and collect the interest** or **spread out the receipt of proceeds** for tax benefits or some other personal financial reason.

Often, though, the seller elects this option simply to help **close the gap** on a sale where the buyer's other financing and available cash fall short of the purchase price.

The **terms of repayment** and the **creation of a security instrument** may be structured in a variety of ways for both **purchase-money mortgages** and a **contract for deed (land contract)**, depending on negotiations between the seller and the buyer.

Sale and leaseback, sale/leaseback, or simply **leaseback** is an arrangement by which a property owner, usually commercial, sells the property to an investor with the understanding that the seller may lease the property from the buyer immediately. This arrangement is often **made to free up capital for use by the former owner**, now the lessee.

Also, in some markets there may be **down payment assistance programs** for certain buyers. Questions linked to this area are most likely to be broad, and simply concentrate on the fact that **first time home buyers**, meaning **those who have not had an ownership interest in a residence within the last three years**, may be eligible for a **home-buyer grant** to help with a down payment.

There are a host of programs and charities that provide this assistance; you should research the ones available in your area in order to better serve both buyers who can use some help and sellers who may expand the prospective buyer pool by sharing this assistance information with them.

IV-C. Government Programs   (Expect 1-2 questions from this area)

Two of the three most common financing methods for institutional lenders are made through the *Federal Housing Administration (FHA)*, and the *Department of Veterans Affairs (VA)*.

FHA loans are residential loans *funded by FHA-approved lenders* but <u>*insured by the FHA*</u>. Both *the borrower* and *the property* must meet FHA guidelines.

FHA loans have a *maximum loan amount* that is *adjusted periodically for <u>local markets</u>*, require a very *low down payment*, often as low as three percent, and are *insured* by an up-front *mortgage insurance premium (MIP)* and periodic *renewal premiums*.

Lenders providing funds for *FHA-insured loans* must follow FHA guidelines in order to ensure that the loan qualifies for FHA approval and backing. Some of these include

- *FHA-approved appraisal*, or *conditional commitment*, on the property, typically requiring that the appraisal be performed by an *FHA-approved appraiser*
- *standards for property condition,* such as construction type and pre-sale repair of property defects
- payment of *an up-front mortgage insurance premium (MIP)*, plus *an annual renewal premium* of one-half of one percent (.5%) of the loan balance; <u>*often the up-front MIP is rolled into the loan total*</u>

Historically, *FHA loans have been assumable*, and most still are, though the rules for assumption have become increasingly stringent.

VA loans are also residential loans *funded by a VA-approved lender* but <u>*a portion of the loan amount is guaranteed* by the government</u>. Like FHA loans, they have guidelines for both the borrower and the property

- VA loans are available for military and ex-military borrowers who qualify for a *certificate of eligibility* from the VA
- the property has to be appraised by the VA and receive a *certificate of reasonable value (CRV)*, which serves as the VA's counterpart to a standard appraisal

Lenders providing funds for *VA-guaranteed loans* must follow VA guidelines in order to ensure that the loan qualifies for VA approval and backing. Some of these include

- use of the *Certificate of Reasonable Value (CRV)*, or 'VA appraisal' for property valuation
- *no prepayment penalty* is allowed
- *assumption rights* -- historically, VA loans have been *assumable*, and most still are, though the rules for assumption have become increasingly stringent

Also, unless the original borrower has received a release of liability from the VA and the lender has accepted it, the borrower remains financially liable to the lender for the loan in the event a subsequent buyer defaults.

The original borrower may also qualify for a restoration of entitlement, allowing full entitlement use on future purchases, if the person assuming the loan is a veteran and substitutes their entitlement for the seller's, or whenever the loan is paid off by either an assuming buyer or the original borrower.

The *Farm Service Agency (FSA)*, formerly the *Farmers Home Administration (FmHA)*, represents another source of *funding for rural, farming, and ranching communities*. FSA provides programs for beginning farmers and ranchers who do not qualify for conventional loans as well as loans to established farmers who have suffered setbacks from natural disasters. *FSA makes direct and guaranteed farm ownership along with business operating loans* to qualified applicants.

If you are planning to enter the real estate business in a rural, farming, or ranching area, you should become familiar with FSA guidelines for qualifying borrowers; however, the particulars are too regional to merit specific questions on the general portion of the exam.

In addition to the government programs above, the following *three major government programs* are involved in the *secondary mortgage market*:

- *Fannie Mae*, the commonly used name for the *Federal National Mortgage Association (FNMA)*,
- *Ginnie Mae*, the commonly used name for the *Government National Mortgage Association (GNMA)*, and
- *Freddie Mac*, the commonly used name for the *Federal Home Loan Mortgage Corporation (FHLMC)*.

Fannie Mae is a corporation chartered by the government to purchase and sell conventional, FHA and VA mortgages in the secondary market; it converts some of its mortgage loans into mortgage-backed securities. It has a set of requirements for the loans it will buy, and has been influential in making mid-range residential mortgages available.

Ginnie Mae is a federally owned corporation that is a division of the *Department of Housing and Urban Development (HUD)*; it works with Fannie Mae to provide a government guarantee for mortgage-backed securities, and underwrites FHA, VA, and certain farmer's home administration loans.

Freddie Mac is the newest of the three, and is a corporation created by Congress to increase the availability of residential financing. It deals primarily in conventional loans, and has strict standardized qualification standards.

IV-D. Mortgages/Deeds of Trust   (Expect 1-2 questions from this area)

Secured instruments for real estate property loans are broadly termed *mortgages*.

A mortgage typically has a *note*, or *promissory note*, which is *the financing instrument* that serves as *evidence of the debt* and *details the terms of repayment*, and the *mortgage*, which is *the security instrument that creates a lien* on the property *as security for the loan*.

A common way of expressing this is that a *borrower secures the note by signing the mortgage*.

The note and the mortgage are two separate documents; the mortgage is typically recorded to assert the encumbrance on the property and is released when the loan is paid off per the terms of the note.

Two key terms for mortgage instruments are

- **hypothecate**, which is *to pledge property as security* for a debt *while retaining possession and use of the property*
- **pledge**, which is to *provide something as security* for a debt, *generally by surrendering possession but not full title*; commonly illustrated by a pawn shop's holding of personal property in exchange for a short-term loan

The two most common ways of structuring mortgages are

- the ordinary **mortgage**, which is a *two-party instrument* between a borrower and an institutional lender. Typically, **the borrower**, or **mortgagor**, pledges the property as security against default and retains the title, and **the lender**, or **mortgagee**, gives the agreed-upon financing for the borrower to acquire the property in exchange for the legal right to force the sale of the property in the event of default.
- a **deed of trust**, or **trust deed**, which is a **three-party instrument** *under which a borrower, known as the* **trustor**, *and an institutional lender, known as the* **beneficiary**, *have a third party, known as the* **trustee**, *hold* **the property's legal title "in trust" until the debt is repaid** *at which time it is conveyed to the property owner; during the repayment period,* **the "owner" holds equitable title**
  - *in the event of default,* **lender foreclosure rights** *under a deed of trust* **are generally nonjudicial**, *or operate without the courts but rather are governed by the financing contract provisions,* **so are more direct** *than under most two-party mortgages, which typically create lien rights requiring court enforcement,* **especially in lien theory states** *(see below)*
  - *since deeds of trust are not in common, conventional use nationwide, they are not likely to be tested in detail, though the terms related to this type of security instrument are quite likely to appear as distractors*

A third common instrument used to provide security in certain seller-financing situations is the **contract for deed**, whereby the seller's security is title retention

- a **contract for deed**, or **land contract**, or **installment contract**, is a **two-party instrument**, typically between the buyer and the seller, under which the seller agrees to accept payments until the purchase price, plus interest, is satisfied, and then to deliver the deed.

  Style note: it is a testing convention to present this as **contract for deed (land contract)**, *though it may appear under any of the terms given above, or even* **installment land sale**.

The following broad differences between mortgages governed by **lien theory**, **title theory**, *and* **intermediary theory** *property laws are presented for information and are not likely to be tested; however, since* **most states have lending and foreclosure laws that favor one over the others**, *the basic concepts are worth noting here.*

- **Lien theory states**, *which are in the majority nationwide, favor lending and foreclosure laws that presume a mortgagor retains both legal and equitable title while the lender simply has a lien interest in the property. In the event of loan default, the lender needs to force a foreclosure sale in order to recover the remaining loan amount; the lender rarely acquires any title interest in the property.*
- **Title theory states** *base their lender's rights in the principle that the lender acquires legal title when the mortgage is executed, but is obligated to return it to the borrower upon full loan repayment. This generally allows for a fairly rapid property possession and foreclosure*

process in the event of mortgage default; in some cases it even legally entitles the lender to full title rights, including all equity, thereby denying the borrower any share in property improvements or appreciation.

- *Intermediate, or hybrid, or modified title theory states take a modified position whereby legal title is held by the borrower barring loan default, which allows it to shift to the lender. Once the lender acquires a title interest, the lender also gains other state-determined title rights, such as the right to sell and/or take possession of the property.*

Another critical area for *general mortgage concepts and terms* has to do some of the more *common clauses or provisions in a financing agreement* that relate to the method, timing, or other details regarding what is required or allowed in a loan repayment. These include

- *alienation clause*, also known as a *due-on-sale clause*, which allows the lender to call the entire *balance of the loan due-and-payable upon the transfer of the property*
- *acceleration clause,* which allows *the lender to call the entire remaining debt due on default*, or after a certain number of consecutive late payments
  - *nonrecourse clause*, or *nonrecourse provision*, which allows the lender to attach only the collateral in the event of default, *leaving all other borrower assets judgment-proof*; this clearly helps protect the borrower's overall interests by *making the loan a specific rather than general lien*
- *defeasance clause*, which requires the lender to provide a *release of mortgage*, or *satisfaction of mortgage*, document when the loan has been repaid; this document can be recorded in the public record to assert that the lien has been removed.
  > *In the case of financing by a deed of trust, this document is known as a release deed, or deed of reconveyance.*
- *assumption clause*, which may be included in a loan document to *either prohibit or allow a borrower to pass along the loan obligation to a subsequent buyer.* In some cases, the original borrower remains liable for the loan in the event the new owner defaults. *But a lender may release the original borrower through*
  - *novation*, which means *substituting one party to a contract for another*, thus releasing the first party from further obligation while shifting that obligation to the new party alone
- *prepayment clause*, or *prepayment penalty clause*, which helps lenders increase their return when a borrower pays off a loan ahead of schedule by charging a fee for early payoffs. *Once quite common*, they are now often subject to regulatory limits, and *are prohibited in some loans*, such as FHA and VA loans.
- *subordination clause*, which serves to clarify that *a loan will accept a subordinate*, or *junior, position* and remain *behind another loan in the priority order of liens*. It is a common clause in second mortgages, although some commercial lenders require borrowers to get existing loan holders to allow their loans to be made secondary to the new loan through a *subordination agreement*.
  - *subrogation, an insurance term regarding an insurance company's right to pay a claim and then collect directly from the responsible party (see Topic Area VIII-A, Title Insurance), may appear as a similar-looking-word type of **distractor for "subordination"***

Other clauses and provisions that arise in financing, and may appear as distractors, include

- **partial release clause**, or **release clause** *(also noted in Topic Area IV-B, Types of Loans, under* **blanket mortgages***)*, which allows a borrower with a single loan covering several properties to sell one, pay off its share to the lender, and receive a release of its property description in the lien from the lender; commonly used by developers when building out a subdivision so they can sell unencumbered properties to purchasers
- **escalation clause,** or **escalator clause,** which may be included in a loan document to **allow the lender to increase the interest rate in the event the borrower makes late payments** or is in default
    - **an escalator clause** *may also refer to* **a clause in leases** *that allows rent changes based on inflation or changing market conditions, such as taxes or operating expenses; when applicable to leases, it will be tested in Topic Area VII-F, Leases*
- **nondisturbance clause,** which may be in a mortgage for properties that are rented, and states that the lender will not terminate leases in the event of foreclosure
    - an **assignment of rents clause** may also be included in mortgages on rental properties to give the lender the right to collect rents directly in the event of borrower default; this assures a lender that a borrower in default does not have long to simply pocket rent money that should be going toward the mortgage

IV-E. Financing/Credit Laws   (Expect 0-2 questions from this area)

There are several federal financing and credit laws that apply to real estate transactions backed by certain government loans.

While it is important for real estate licensees to be familiar with the main provisions of the following laws, the more intricate details are better left to tests for professional lenders than those for entry-level real estate licensees. Also note that there are mandatory disclosures involved with each one and that these are testable material, especially since you should be familiar with what lenders are supposed to provide to your clients.

Remember as you read through the details of the following six federal laws, you should expect to see at most two questions on all of this material, and the questions should test the most relevant and appropriate facts that an entry level licensee ought to know.

The primary financing and credit laws include
- **Truth in Lending Act (TILA)** and **Regulation Z**
- **Real Estate Settlement Procedures Act (RESPA)** and **Regulation X**
- **Dodd-Frank Act/TILA-RESPA Integrated Disclosure Rule (TRID)**
- **Equal Credit Opportunity Act (ECOA)**
- **Fair Credit Reporting Act**
- **Homeowner's Protection Act of 1998,** also known as the **Private Mortgage Insurance (PMI) Act**

The federal **Truth in Lending Act (TILA)**, a part of the **Consumer Credit Protection Act**, has a detailed set of loan **disclosure** and **advertising** requirements for lenders who originate residential loans. **Regulation Z** is the regulation that implements TILA and explains how lenders are to comply with those parts of TILA that bear on consumer credit.

Since TILA and Regulation Z relate primarily to loan advertisements and disclosures, they will be presented more fully in Topic Area IX-C, Advertising.

The **Real Estate Settlement Procedures Act (RESPA)** is a critical federal law that governs lender practices, often in connection with the **Truth in Lending Act (Regulation Z)**.

Regulation X is the regulation that implements RESPA; they are often presented together as RESPA (Regulation X).

RESPA requirements apply to most loans on one-to-four family residential properties, specifically when they involve a **federally related residential mortgage loan in any lien position**, including many home purchase loans, refinances, lender-approved assumptions, property improvement loans, **home equity lines of credit (HELOC)**, and **reverse mortgages**.

First passed in 1974, RESPA is a consumer protection statute that was **initially implemented and enforced by** the **Department of Housing and Urban Development (HUD)**, but the **Dodd-Frank Wall Street Reform and Consumer Protection Act (Dodd-Frank Act) of 2010** shifted these responsibilities to the **Consumer Financial Protection Bureau (CFPB)**.

The purposes of RESPA are
- **to help consumers become better shoppers** for **settlement services**
- **to eliminate kickbacks and referral fees** that unnecessarily increase the costs of certain settlement services

RESPA requires that borrowers receive certain specific **disclosures** at various times in the loan process. These include
- **costs** associated with settlement
- **lender practices** in loan servicing and **impound/escrow accounts**
  - **impound/escrow accounts** for paying taxes, insurance, and other routine charges **are limited** to a 'cushion' of funds equivalent to **approximately two months' worth of prorated annual expenses**
- **business relationships** between **settlement service providers (SSPs)**, formerly referred to as **Controlled Business Arrangements (CBAs)**, more recently revised to **Affiliated Business Arrangements (AfBAs)**

Under **TILA-RESPA Integrated Documentation (TRID)** rules, which began in late 2015 due to the **CFPB**'s **"Know Before You Owe"** efforts to enhance consumer awareness through providing greater transparency to the mortgage and closing process, the following required documents and procedures are now common in residential lending, **though not applicable to all RESPA-covered consumer loans.**
- a single **Loan Estimate (LE)** of settlement costs replaces the **(1) Good Faith Estimate (GFE)** of settlement charges and **(2) Truth-in-Lending (TIL) Disclosure Statement (preliminary)** of total loan costs
  - **LEs** must be provided **within three business days of receiving basic applicant information**
  - **applicants do not have to provide income verification** in order to get an LE
  - **applicants can request LEs from multiple lenders** for comparison purposes
  - **LEs** represent financial data, **NOT a commitment to lend**

- a new *Closing Disclosure (CD) statement* replaces the *HUD-1* and *TIL Disclosure Statement (final)* of total loan costs
  - *a CD* must be provided to consumers *at least three business days before closing*

These changes will be in the lender's court, but you need to keep abreast of new requirements and help consumers bridge the difference between the old and new procedures that lenders must observe when processing transaction documents.

Also, the one-or-two questions that you MAY see on the test will reference TRID or the specific forms mentioned above if they are based on the new procedures; more detail than that provided above is too lender-specific to be tested on an entry-level salesperson exam.

However, it will be professionally important to learn more about TRID to ensure you can understand and explain this part of a real estate transaction.

TRID has streamlined the disclosure documentation for many residential loan transactions, primarily by replacing some forms required at loan application and at closing with simpler ones.

Certain loans, though, such as applicable HELOCS and reverse mortgages, must continue to use existing TIL and RESPA forms, including the HUD-1 Settlement Statement.

HUD-1 is a standard form that clearly shows all charges imposed on borrowers and sellers in connection with the settlement. It has been used nationwide for loan transactions covered by RESPA to make loan information uniform for ease in the secondary market, and is often used for other transactions as well due to its acceptability as a standard form for recording closing costs and proceeds.

In addition, at the time of loan application, a lender must give an applicant for financing a RESPA-covered residential property exempt from TRID with the following documents

- *Good Faith Estimate (GFE) of settlement costs*, which lists the charges the buyer is likely to pay at settlement; *this is only an estimate and the actual charges may differ*
- *Mortgage Servicing Disclosure Statement*, which discloses to the borrower whether the lender intends to service the loan or transfer it to another lender
- *Special Information Booklet*, which contains consumer information regarding various real estate settlement services

If these are not given at the time of application, the lender must mail them within three days unless the loan is turned down within that time.

The federal *Equal Credit Opportunity Act (ECOA) requires lenders to ignore the following factors about an applicant* when reviewing a credit application

- *race*
- *color*
- *religion*
- *national origin*
- *sex*
- *marital status*
- *age (over the age of majority)*
- *receipt of income from public assistance programs, such as food stamps*

- ***has exercised, in good faith, any right under the Consumer Credit Protection Act***

This list has many of the same protected groups as those in federal Fair Housing law, but ***the last four categories are unique ECOA protected groups*** for borrowers.

The federal ***Fair Credit Reporting Act (1970)*** is designed to protect consumers from inaccurate credit reporting by ensuring the right of consumers to ***inspect their credit reports*** and ***make corrections or attach explanations*** where necessary.

The Act also requires lenders to ***notify an applicant which reporting agency's report it used*** in the event a lender's review of a credit report prompted the lender to decide ***to deny credit***.

The ***Homeowner's Protection Act of 1998***, or the ***Private Mortgage Insurance (PMI) Act*** is a federal act that applies to many ***high LTV*** loans originated after July 29, 1999. According to the PMI Act, since PMI only covers the 'top' of the loan, it generally does not even apply once the loan's balance drops below an LTV of 80 percent. Therefore the PMI Act requires

- ***PMI coverage and payments to terminate automatically once the mortgage has amortized to 78 percent of the original value of the property*** if the borrower is current on all mortgage payments and does not have a government-defined "high-risk" loan
- ***the lender must tell the borrower at closing when the mortgage will hit that mark***

*The PMI Act was enacted in response to abuse in the PMI market. Historically, and still, lenders making high LTV **conventional loans** typically require the borrower to protect the lender against default by purchasing **PMI**.*

***PMI policies cover the portion of the loan amount that is at greatest risk for the lender**, and **generally cover no more than the top 30 percent of the loan amount** against default, thereby lowering the lender's risk and allowing them to lend upwards of 95 percent LTV.*

Unfortunately, since PMI premiums are relatively small and most borrowers are unaware of PMI's limited coverage, it long went unnoticed when unscrupulous lenders collected them for the life of the loan, even though the coverage ceased to apply after the first few years.

This too-widespread practice prompted the development of the PMI Act as a federal protection for homeowners.

*Also, though **some state and regional conventions use MIP and PMI interchangeably**, generally **MIP refers to FHA's up-front mortgage insurance** requirements and **PMI** refers to insurance required by other lenders **that is billed as a line-item, like taxes, in the monthly payment for PITI**.*

As anyone who has read a newspaper within the past few years will know, ***mortgage fraud*** has been big news nationwide, and often "local players" are being not only found out, but caught, convicted, and written up in local papers with surprising regularity.

Despite the impact of mortgage fraud being so widespread and significant, for entry-level exam purposes it will suffice to recognize examples of what constitutes fraud rather than delving into the particulars of government oversight or enforcement.

*However, the **definition of mortgage fraud is worth noting**, since the correct answer to any test question that starts, **"Which of the following situations BEST represents mortgage fraud?"** will rely on the following*

- ***Mortgage fraud is a material misstatement, misrepresentation, or omission*** relating to the property or potential mortgage ***relied on by an underwriter or lender*** to fund, purchase or insure a loan. [emphases added]

*More for the sake of the "big picture" than for exam questions, though, it is worth knowing that the **Federal Bureau of Investigation (FBI) investigates mortgage fraud**, generally under **federal mail fraud and wire fraud statutes**, since all plans to defraud lenders rely at some point in the process on mail/courier services and/or wire transfers.*

*The FBI, which widely publishes the definition of mortgage fraud given above, also distinguishes between **two types of mortgage fraud***

- ***fraud for profit**, which is generally planned and executed by someone to profit financially from the sale proceeds, such as arranging a large loan based on inflated appraisals and then simply defaulting after pocketing any surplus funds*
- ***fraud for housing**, which generally refers to **a borrower who provides false financial information** to qualify for a loan and use the property as a primary residence, typically with the intent of repaying the loan*
    - *this type of fraud is commonly discovered when the borrower cannot keep up payments and the property goes into foreclosure*

*A more recent federal law, the **Fraud Enforcement and Recovery Act of 2009** or **FERA**, is intended to enhance enforcement of mortgage fraud cases, but should not appear on the test.*

*So, despite having given rise to so many complications in the housing market during recent years, **mortgage fraud is primarily a matter for lenders**.*

*However, **all real estate licensees should see the warning signs** when working with either buyers or sellers, **and refuse to take any part in either encouraging or ignoring them**.*

According to the following FBI warning, doing so could allow various parties in a transaction to risk having a life-changing encounter with the law:

> **Mortgage Fraud is investigated by the Federal Bureau of Investigation and is punishable by up to 30 years in federal prison or $1,000,000 fine, or both. It is illegal for a person to make any false statement regarding income, assets, debt, or matters of identification, or to willfully overvalue any land or property, in a loan and credit application for the purpose of influencing in any way the action of a financial institution.**

Predatory lending is distinct from mortgage fraud because it primarily affects borrowers rather than lending institutions. ***Unfair, deceptive, fraudulent, abusive repayment arrangements***: these are all terms associated with predatory lending.

Some of the more apparent examples of predatory lending are seen in "loan shark" fast-cash loans with a high repayment, often arranged informally between individual parties, as well as in credit card arrangements that allow issuers to charge a 25+% APR for cash advances along with imposing high late-payment fees while boosting the APR, often by more than double the original rate, after one or two late payments.

But for real estate financing, it is commonly tied to ***unscrupulous mortgage lending practices*** that take advantage of borrowers, notably subprime borrowers, by such tactics as

- *excessive or unnecessary loan preparation fees*
- *building hidden fees into the loan itself*
- *not fully disclosing or explaining risks, such as adjustable interest rate adjustments*

*Ultimately, the **financial abuse of a borrower through predatory lending** may occur at any point in the mortgage process **from up-front charges right through all of the foreclosure costs** that borrowers would never have incurred had they not been granted a loan they could not afford. Many **abuses that may occur during the mortgage servicing process** may be categorized separately by the term **predatory mortgage servicing**.*

Parties to the lending process for residential properties include the following individuals and/or institutions

- *mortgage lender* refers to any institution or investment entity that provides mortgage funds
- *underwriter* ultimately refers *to the lender/lending institution* that reviews and approves loan applications, though *the process is generally administered by one or more employees* of the lender who use that term as their job title
- *loan originator*, or *mortgage loan originator*, is any person who *takes, offers, or negotiates terms of a residential mortgage loan application for compensation or gain*
- *mortgage broker* is another name for a loan originator, *though in practice it may further indicate one who employs other loan originators; overall, **a mortgage broker is characterized as a professional that helps borrowers successfully locate funding sources and secure funds***

One of the government responses to the recent mortgage crisis was the passage of a federal law, the ***Secure and Fair Enforcement for Mortgage Licensing Act (SAFE) of 2008***, that began requiring *loan originators* to comply with the following conditions

1. complete 20 hours of *prelicensing education*
2. *pass a state-administered examination*
3. complete eight hours of *continuing education (CE) annually*, and
4. *maintain professional registration* through the ***Nationwide Mortgage Licensing System and Registry (NMLSR)***

***SAFE** is part of the **Housing and Economic Recovery Act** and sets forth education, testing, and other standards, including mandatory registration and **state licensing** of mortgage loan originators through NMLSR.*

The most obvious part of this consumer protection effort is to ensure that individual loan originators are uniformly educated, tested, and licensed before practicing.

Further, each licensee receives a unique identifier that would make it more difficult for those who would prey on the public to "disappear" across state lines and resume business undetected.

In fact, the Act is designed to afford consumers easy access to a loan originator's employment history and record of past disciplinary or enforcement actions, regardless of where the loan originator has lived or worked, or how many times the individual has moved around the country.

This ends the presentation of key terms and concepts likely to be either tested or used as distractors in this Content Outline Section.

V-A. Nature of Agency Relationships (Expect 2-3 questions from this area)

Common law broadly refers to the body of "general" laws that are based on custom, conventions, and case law, or ***"judges' law,"*** rather than statutory or civil law. The ***common law of agency*** refers to the category of common law that ***applies to relationships and responsibilities created when one person acts as a representative for another.***

> *Agency relationships and terminology* have been the subject of great discussion and state-specific legislation nationwide for over fifteen years.

> *This entire Content Outline Topic Area provides a broad treatment of agency relationships based on the **common law of agency**. Many of the terms and definitions found in common law have been adopted by many jurisdictions in their statutes and administrative policies.*

> ***State-specific terms, definitions, and applications of agency may also be tested on the state portion of the exam.*** *Further, if some terms below do not appear in your state's agency law, or are defined differently there, they still represent basic, general knowledge that may be presented and tested on the general portion of the exam as common law.*

> ***Because so many states have adopted agency statutes, you may see essentially the same questions on both the general and the state-specific portion of the exam.*** *It is important to remember that when that happens, it often means that a state's statutes or policies were enacted to allow licensing officials to act directly, swiftly, and often quite severely to punish licensees who violate agency responsibilities.*

>> *Therefore, the Sample Exam at the end of this book will include the qualifying phrase **"according to the common law of agency"** wherever necessary to clarify that the intent of the question draws on common law for its answer.*

>> *However, PSI may not yet be doing the same, so **think of that phrase whenever you see an agency question on the general portion of the licensing exam.***

>> ***While taking the test,*** *set aside legal nitpicking and **assume that the principles of common law are implicit in <u>general</u> questions,** and that they remain valid despite state-specific differences in terminology, definitions, or application. After all, you are in "the testing state," NOT your home state, so think past the border; this is especially true in Oklahoma, which has a special notice on its PSI bulletin about precisely this distinction!*

>> *And keep this thought firmly in mind, too: Your ticket to passing the test lies in remembering that despite whether or not you like a particular question, one of the four choices will give you one more point toward a passing grade – so find it!*

Under the common law of agency, which serves as a starting point for state-specific agency laws and regulations, the definitions of the primary terms that identify the ***parties*** and ***their functions in agency relationships*** include

- ***an agent***, who is authorized to act on behalf of another (generally the principal) and bind them by the agent's decisions and actions; also known as a ***fiduciary***, or ***person in a position of trust***
- ***a principal***, who grants the authority for another to act on their behalf

- *a subagent*, who acts as an agent of an agent
- *a customer*, who is not in an agency relationship with a licensee
- *a client*, who is in an agency relationship with a licensee, generally as a principal
- *an attorney-in-fact*, who is any person, not necessarily a lawyer, who has been granted a *power of attorney (POA)* to act on behalf of someone else
- *a proxy*, who is a stand-in for another and has limited, generally very temporary authority; can be loosely used to mean agent

The nature of agency relationships, regardless of whether an agent is working for one or both parties in a transaction, requires adhering to a variety of *professional and ethical expectations* which are typically guided by a set of *fiduciary responsibilities*.

Fiduciary is the term for the position of *trust* that marks an agent/principal relationship: the principal trusts the agent to 'do right.' But 'doing right' involves some common legal requirements and obligations, most notably adhering to *basic fiduciary duties* such as *loyalty*, *obedience*, *accounting*, *disclosure*, and *confidence*.

> *Each of these terms has a specific meaning under the common law of agency; some also go by other legally synonymous names. And many respected lawyers, textbook authors, and classroom instructors would supplement this list. These terms will be explained in Topic Area V-C, Agency Duties.*

Though licensees acting as agents have specific fiduciary duties to a client, *they always owe* the obligations of *honesty and fair dealing* to all parties, *including customers*.

Types of agency differ depending on the *extent of an agent's authority*, which ranges from being *specific to one issue or transaction* right *up to being unlimited*. The following are three broad categories of agent authority within agency relationships

- *universal*, which grants the agent the authority to *represent the principal in all matters*; this may be exemplified by the authority given someone who has been granted an unlimited power of attorney in both personal and business matters
- *general*, which grants the agent *broad authority to act continuously on behalf of the principal in all authorized business matters*, such as *a licensee affiliated with a broker/agent* or *a property manager acting on behalf of a landlord*
  > *Note: Though Black's Law Dictionary identifies this term as synonymous with universal agency, many real estate textbooks distinguish between them, limiting general agency to the range of ongoing responsibilities and authority contained in a particular employer/employee relationship, so look for this distinction in test questions.*
- *special*, which means the agent's authority to represent the principal is more restricted than general agency, and typically is *limited to a particular transaction*, such as *a listing*

Types of agency relationships vary depending on who the agent represents in a transaction; the most common *types of agency representation* and *terms for the agent* include

- *single agency*, which means that the agent is representing only one party, buyer or seller, in a transaction
  - *seller's broker*, or *seller's agent*, which means the type of single agency in which the agent is representing the seller, *typically as a listing agent*

- **buyer's broker**, or **buyer's agent**, which means the type of single agency in which the agent is representing the buyer
- **dual agency**, which means the agent is a **dual agent**, and **represents both parties**
  Note: <u>disclosure</u> of dual agency status has always been a good idea, but is becoming a requirement in an increasing number of states.
- **subagency**, which means anyone who is authorized to act as an agent for the agent of a principal, in other words, 'below' the primary agent as a **subagent**

*Note: for many decades, many licensees who were working with buyers were <u>technically</u> working <u>for</u> the seller as a subagent of listing brokers through membership in a **multiple listing service (MLS)**.*

*To avoid genuine and perceived **conflicts of interest**, the vast majority of states have legislated state-specific applications of agency law. Some have gone so far as to leave the terms 'subagency/subagent' out of their list of agency relationships to avoid linking it with its former 'automatic' creation. The concept and basic relationship, though, still survive.*

*In many states, there are now **restrictions on the automatic subagency** of the primary broker and affiliated licensees, and the broker may assign a **designated agent**, or **transaction agent**, to be the only one in the office who is working for a particular client.*

*Other states recognize **transaction brokers**, or **intermediaries**, or **facilitators**, who are not agent-advocates for either party, but act in a professionally prudent manner for both parties while performing **ministerial**, or administrative, tasks in the course of a transaction.*

As you can see from comparing the above to your state-specific prelicensing study materials, agency issues, though rooted in the common law of agency, vary considerably in definition and application from state to state.

Once you are licensed, you will undoubtedly be expected to keep up with your state's agency terms, definitions, relationships, disclosure policies and forms, and changes through taking continuing education courses for license renewal.

V-B. Creation and Disclosure of Agency and Agency Agreements (General)
[Regulatory Details in State Portion] (Expect 2-4 questions from this area)

The **creation of agency relationships** occurs in a variety of ways: they may be created by **express** agreements, either written or oral, or **implied** by the actions of the parties.

An express relationship means that the parties have a **definite oral or actual written mutual understanding** of their representation relationship
- **listing agreements** and **property management agreements** represent the most common examples of **express agency contracts**, since they clearly identify the principal and the agent, and their mutual obligations and responsibilities

An implied relationship means that *the actions of the parties suggest there is a representation understanding between them*, as when a licensee and a potential buyer have visited several properties together but have not yet discussed or executed an agency representation agreement

- *family members, former clients,* and *friends* represent three categories of potential clients that may have *an automatic implied agency with a licensee*, so are subject to creating *misunderstandings about actual agency representation – these people are likely to show up in test questions*, and *in practice are best handled with a written representation agreement*

*In cases where a licensee is representing a family member in a real estate transaction, the most ethical course is to inform all parties, preferably in writing, of the family relationship. This will also serve to protect the licensee against legal action for **nondisclosure of a potential conflict of interest** should other parties in the transaction find out later and feel they were mistreated.*

*Terms like **ostensible agency**, or **agency by ratification**, or **agency by estoppel** are related to the above terms and **may show up as distractors**, but are too legally technical for entry-level testing, or quick explanation here.*

Agency employment contract is the increasingly widespread term for the most common **agency agreement**, the time-honored **listing agreement**, since this term encompasses other, newer representation arrangements such as **buyer representation** and **dual representation**. It also clarifies the agreement's status as an **employment contract that specifies the licensee's duties, obligations, agency relationship, and compensation arrangements**.

As indicated in the Topic Area heading, details of agency disclosure requirements are almost exclusively governed by state-specific statutes.

*Questions in this area will rely on information provided in the other Topic Areas in this Section, and probably include scenario-type questions **illustrating or exploring issues related to the explanation and disclosure of agency relationships** as well as any **licensee disclosure of pre-contract-signing interest in a property**, such as buying or selling a property for a relative, friend, business associate, or the licensee personally.*

State-specific regulations often define events that create agency relationships, e.g., "upon signing an employment contract," or trigger mandatory disclosure of agency relationships, e.g., "at first substantive contact." These phrases and similar language are now common in state agency laws, but state-specific language should not appear on this portion of the test.

Remember that questions from this Topic Area need to be correct based on either common law of agency or basic contract law.

So, as noted in other Topic Areas for Agency, if the focus of information in those Topic Areas is disclosure, it will most likely be tallied here even though it was discussed elsewhere within the Content Outline.

However, this Topic Area may include **application questions** that **illustrate or explore issues related to the types of agency and fiduciary obligations** defined above, as well as **examples of licensee and agent conduct and obligation to various parties in real estate transactions**.

Some questions are likely to present *examples of licensee conduct* in relation to *principals, clients, customers,* and *members of the public.*

Agency duties would include questions about licensees' *disclosure of any conflict of interest*, such as informing a principal of an agent's personal interest before buying or selling something for themselves, their family, their friends, or their business associates.

> *Self-dealing* is a term that describes a situation in which an agent breaches a fiduciary trust while pursuing the agent's own personal interest at the expense of the principal's best interests.

> *One of the many, many examples of self-dealing would be for a licensee to take a listing, convince the principal to sell for a below-market price either to the agent personally or an associate, and soon thereafter resell the property at its actual value and pocket the profit.*

V-C. Responsibilities of Agent/Principal (Expect 2-4 questions from this area)

An agent acting as a fiduciary and an agent's basic fiduciary duties were noted above in Topic Area V-A, Nature of Agency Relationships; they will be explained in more detail below and most likely be tallied for testing in this Topic Area.

The nature of agency relationships, regardless of whether an agent is working for either or both parties in a transaction, requires adhering to a variety of *professional and ethical expectations* which are typically guided by common law *fiduciary responsibilities*.

> *Fiduciary* is the term for the position of *trust* that marks an agent/principal relationship: the principal trusts the agent to 'do right.' But 'doing right' involves some common legal requirements and obligations, most notably
> - *loyalty*, or *allegiance*, which means to steadfastly work for, never against, the best interests of the principal while applying expected, *reasonable care, skill, and diligence* in the performance of all transaction-related matters
> - *obedience*, which means to adhere to the principal's instructions, but *does NOT include illegal actions*
> - *accounting*, which means to give a fair and accurate accounting of all funds that are transaction-related, *even if that means after the transaction is over and the agency relationship has been terminated*
> - *disclosure*, which means to disclose all pertinent information *to the principal*
> - *confidence*, which means to keep confidential all information that might weaken the principal's interests, such as lowest acceptable price or unusual/extenuating circumstances. *Note, though, these conditions regarding confidentiality:*
>   - confidential information *may* be revealed *with the principal's permission only*
>   - this obligation *does NOT apply to illegal information*, such as material property conditions, which *MUST be disclosed* to other parties
>   - *confidentiality outlives the termination of the agency relationship*, which means an agent is bound to maintain indefinitely the confidentiality of information acquired in the course of the transaction; *some states allow licensees to disclose confidential information without legal liability for breaching a fiduciary duty*

when necessary in the course of a real estate commission investigation into complaints against the licensee

*The fiduciary duties given above are often presented in classes and textbooks along with an acronym as a memory aid; sometimes this is "COALD," though some publishers use "COLAD" instead. Both refer to **Confidentiality**, **Obedience**, **Accounting**, **Loyalty**, and **Disclosure**. If this helps you, use the one you like, or learned in class, or made up yourself!*

As noted above, the fiduciary responsibility of **confidentiality outlives the termination of an agency relationship**, as does **final accounting** for funds – this Topic Area is the most likely place to find questions on which responsibilities outlast the termination of agency.

As a fiduciary, the agent who accepts earnest money has an obligation of **accounting**, which means the agent is obligated to avoid either of the following situations with transaction-related funds

- **commingling**, which means mingling, or combining, transaction funds with other funds that are required to be maintained separately; this could result from putting the funds in the wrong account, either business or personal
- **conversion**, which refers to **converting funds to another use than the one intended by the principal**, or **misappropriating them**, as in using earnest money to pay office expenses **or for any personal use**; conversion is generally preceded by commingling

*Additional particulars regarding the **handling of earnest money**, such as **to whom it is given**, **into which account it gets deposited**, the **time period within which it must be deposited**, and **method(s) of disbursal, especially when there is a dispute**, are all state-specific and may be tested on the state portion of the exam.*

Remember that even though licensees have specific fiduciary duties to a client, they owe the obligations of **honesty and fair dealing** to all parties, **including customers**.

Conflict of interest is an especially delicate—and litigious—prospect within any **dual agency relationship**, since a licensee representing both parties has unusual restrictions on every fiduciary duty, most notably **loyalty**, **confidence**, and **disclosure**.

*In general, dual agency imposes obvious **constraints on disclosures of confidential material known about either party**, and conflicts over "full" representation to each arise easily. For example, if a dual agent's keeping the confidence of a seller's motivation from the buyer hurts the buyer's ability to negotiate a lower price, the buyer may feel cheated, perhaps enough to sue.*

Some lawyers—and real estate instructors—doubt the basic validity of "dual agency": they argue it is a legal impossibility to act as a true fiduciary for opposing parties. They might even suggest it would be prudent for each party to engage separate lawyers and simply let the "dual agent" licensee play messenger and handle the transaction paperwork. All of this is way too advanced for testing, but illustrates how even "basic" dual agency is anything but simple.

Those states that formally recognize dual agency have their own legal positions, definitions, guidelines, and regulations. All of these are tied closely to honest and fair dealing, and generally require getting written agreements before sharing sensitive, especially confidential, information.

All questions on dual agency on this part of the exam will be based in the broadest application of common law; more detailed questions will be on the state-specific portion, if applicable.

While misunderstandings arise all the time in the course of a transaction, when an agent, or another party, creates them through *making representations* involving *puffery*, *misrepresentation*, or *fraud*, whenever they are found out, before or after closing, litigation may not be far behind. The basic meaning of these terms includes

- *puffing*, or *puffery*, which refers to any general exaggeration found in promotional materials or agent comments intended to create a stronger impression of a property
- *misrepresentation* means any variety of misleading statements or undisclosed facts that an agent reasonably should have known and disclosed
    - *negligent misrepresentation*, which means making a careless statement where the exercise of due diligence and professional standards of care would have made the correct facts known
    - *material misrepresentation*, which means making a false statement – or failing to make a known, material disclosure – that is likely to induce a reasonable party to act against that party's own best interest
- *fraud* means intentional misrepresentation designed to persuade a party to make a decision the party would not have made had full and accurate disclosure been made

Where the line is drawn along the scale to distinguish one from the other among these terms, especially between misrepresentation and fraud, is often subjective and settled in court, where it generally rests on degree of knowledge and intent of the agent, and injury to the party suffering damages.

V-D. Responsibilities of Agent to Customers and Third Parties, including Disclosure, Honesty, Integrity, Accounting for Money   (Expect 1-2 questions from this area)

As noted repeatedly for the sake of its importance: even though licensees have specific fiduciary duties to a client, they owe the obligations of *honesty and fair dealing* to all parties, *including customers.*

*So, expect at least one question on this crucial point, and perhaps a second that presents a scenario in which a licensee's behavior toward unrepresented parties in a transaction applies this principle as **the best response**, though it will almost certainly either upset a client or be less lucrative. And, obviously, full and timely accounting for money is always not show professional integrity, but is generally also legally required.*

V-E. Termination of Agency   (Expect 1-2 questions from this area)

An agency relationship is *terminated* for any of a number of reasons, all of which fall under the broad labels of *operation of law* or *acts of parties*.

Operation of law refers to legally *"automatic" mechanisms*, such as when a contract is terminated upon the discovery of the lack of one or more necessary elements, as when a party does not actually have legal authority to enter into a contract in the first place, or when a contingency date is not met.

*Such a contract termination is typically automatic due to existing laws requiring sufficient legal elements for it to remain in force. **The operation of law is often passive**, which means it occurs without active intervention, such as when a deadline passes, or someone forgets Valentine's Day.*

*Note: PSI's Expanded Outline refers to operation of law as **force of law**, so expect to see that term rather than the one more commonly used. **Force of law** is generally used to identify **the legal authority to compel an event**, typically one unwanted by at least one party involved, such as a foreclosure, prescriptive easement, or the exercise of eminent domain. By contrast, **operation of law covers many administrative events**, such as the release of obligations at the end of a contract period, or the termination of legal liability after any applicable statute of limitations runs out.*

Other commonplace occurrences that terminate contracts based on the operation of law include
- *completion* of the transaction through *performance*, or *fulfillment*, of contract elements
- *expiration* of the agency period
- *lack of legal elements* in the original contract, such as finding that the contract was made for an illegal purpose or that the "principal" lacked the legal capacity to create the contract

Acts of parties that can serve to terminate a contract generally include such circumstances as
- *mutual agreement* of the parties
- *revocation* of contract by the principal/client; as a unilateral act, it may incur liability for the client if it is successfully contested by the agent
- *renunciation* or *abandonment* of contract by the agent; like revocation, since it is a unilateral act, it may incur liability for the agent and/or brokerage if it is successfully contested by the principal/client
- *breach of contract* by one of the parties, which generally incurs liability for the party in breach

Listing agreements, like other agency agreements, may be terminated for reasons provided above. In addition to those factors, though, the following reasons may also provide grounds for terminating a listing
- *bankruptcy* of either party
- *loss of title by seller* through tax sale, foreclosure, or other legal action
- *condemnation* of the property under an eminent domain proceeding
- *destruction* of the listed property
- *death or incapacity* of one of the parties
- *revocation* of agreement by the principal, which may make the principal liable for breach of contract
- *renunciation* of agreement or *abandonment of agency services* by the agent, which may make the agent liable for breach of contract

Most of the questions on agency relationships will be broad, such as listing several events and asking which one triggers the creation or termination of a particular type of agency, or which of several definitions best fits a particular type of agency.

This ends the presentation of key terms and concepts likely to be either tested or used as distractors in this Content Outline Section.

VI. Property Condition and Disclosures   (8 questions)
(5 Topic Areas; 19 Sub-Topics—each will be covered in its respective Topic Area)

VI-A. Property Condition Disclosure   (Expect 1-2 questions from this area)

Though disclosure of property condition is a sound, ethical business practice that will limit a licensee's future liability in the event of post-sale discovery of defects, there are no federal requirements or standard forms for these disclosures.

However, the **Residential Lead-Based Paint Hazard Reduction Act of 1992** requires including a **lead-based paint disclosure notice either in or with sales contracts for residential properties built prior to 1978**, the year lead-based paint was banned.

*Questions in this area will most likely be based on this requirement or else present a scenario in which the licensee's **disclosure of material facts and/or known defects** will be the best answer.*

Despite there being no federal forms or requirements, an increasing number of states have developed a standardized form and specific regulations governing their use in residential real estate transactions.

These forms are commonly controlled by state requirements, and generally require the seller to complete them without the assistance of the licensee.

*Further, in the event a seller misrepresents the property's condition, there may still be **liabilities for the licensee in accepting the seller's self-reporting** without performing a due diligence review and confirmation of the seller's statements.*

VI-B. Warranties   (Expect 0-1 question from this area)

Home warranties, or **home protection plans**, are a **type of insurance** that generally have a one-year contract period and cover service and/or replacement costs for major systems, such as heating/cooling, ducts, hot water heater, electrical, and plumbing. They also cover major appliances, such as range, refrigerator, dishwasher, washer/dryer, ceiling fans, and garage door openers.

The details of coverage and cost vary depending on the number of insurers, if any, in a particular market, and the specific coverages offered.

A basic warranty policy may cost a few hundred dollars, and can be paid for by either party.

*Often a seller offers it as part of the contract in order to both demonstrate good faith and avoid after-closing problems with a buyer over the normal wear-and-tear failure of a covered system or appliance. **Most plans provide coverage even during the listing period**, so can be a seller's hedge against expensive surprises even while the property is on the market.*

If a listing does not offer a home protection plan, the buyer may either request one as a contract condition or purchase one as a new homeowner.

Regardless of which party pays, it is a useful service to the buyer to have information on these potentially major-expense saving policies available, if only because a warranty may also save the agent from angry calls from a buyer after closing regarding appliance or system failures.

Questions on these policies will be broad, since they are neither available nor uniform in coverages or prices in different markets.

*Questions on home warranties may also focus on **the important principle that licensees should provide information and choices, not conclusions or particular-company recommendations, on this and other professional services**.*

In the course of a real estate transaction, if a licensee steers a client to a particular company or professional for any service when there are a variety from which to choose, there are possible strong consequences for the licensee from both a dissatisfied client and competing service providers.

VI-C. Need for Inspection and Obtaining/Verifying Information
(Expect 1-3 questions from this area)

A licensee has an obligation to perform a ***due diligence property inspection and verification of information*** in order to ***discover material facts and/or defects*** that the ***licensee reasonably should have known about***.

This due diligence verification also applies to researching and ***confirming, or correcting, property data*** supplied by the owner or the owner's agent.

This generally involves reviewing information in ***the public record***, such as ***assessment data*** on ***annual taxes***, ***lot size and dimensions***, ***total square footage of any buildings***, ***zoning type and applicable restrictions***, as well as other general property expenses, such as utilities and heating/cooling costs.

In the course of verifying information, a licensee may see ***adverse consequences*** or "red flags" to property data that the seller will have to be prepared to address, either in price concessions or other remedies; ***it is essential for the licensee to discuss these with principals,*** *and, while observing the duty of honest and fair dealing, direct non-clients making inquiries on property matters to their own transaction representatives for answers.*

*For example, if the property is in a **flood zone** that requires special insurance, a seller will have to recognize that the cost of ownership for a new buyer may be higher than the buyer thought, and may use that expense and risk to justify a low-ball offer.*

In an actual instance, a seller had a combined residential and commercial operation that got sold to a buyer who continued the commercial operation only to have it shut down by a zoning enforcement officer's cease and desist order. As it happened, the property was not zoned for the previous owner's commercial activity, so continuing it represented an illegal activity. After suing the seller and the seller's broker for misrepresentation, the buyer went to the local zoning authority about this matter, and ultimately the property's commercial use was approved.

In this case, had the listing licensee confirmed the property's zoning classification, the seller could have either sought the zoning change or provided prospective buyers with accurate information and let them pursue a change.

Or a licensee may see unexploited property **opportunities** in zoning possibilities.

*For example, if the property is three acres with one house on it and its zoning classification requires one acre to build, an owner may want to consider **subdividing** the property and selling it in pieces. Or pricing and marketing the property for its subdivision potential, leaving the option to subdivide to the buyer.*

Also, for properties in **subdivisions** this means getting a copy of the **subdivision CCRs**, and for **common interest ownership properties**, this means getting the **homeowners' association rules** or comparable documents **and confirming all association fees**.

Incorrect or approximated property information needs to either be corrected or **disclosed as unverified** in order to provide notice to interested parties that the data is subject to change when verified by closer research, inspection, or measurement.

Even though an attorney or title company is likely to provide a **title search** in the course of the transaction, it is prudent to at least check the ownership/deed records under the name of the "owner." *(Title searches will be detailed in Topic Area VIII-A, Title Insurance.)*

As noted in an earlier Section, a listing licensee in South Carolina was sued by a would-have-been buyer for not having discovered that the "seller" only had a life estate interest in the property. Regardless of what this interest means, this could have been avoided if the licensee had either checked the public records or requested, and then read, a title report.

Due diligence verification can also include matters related to requesting, interpreting, and explaining professional **appraisals**, **surveys**, **home inspections**, **property inspection reports**, or other tests, such as **tests of well water purity**, **soil contamination**, **septic tank condition** and **soil percolation**, or the age, location, and condition of **underground storage tanks** for home heating oil.

In the event of **nondisclosure of material facts and/or defects**, the seller and all of the seller's agents may incur **legal liability and various penalties**, depending on a court's finding of fault.

*While this standard of care may extend to **discovering stigmatizing conditions**, specific **disclosures** are either **governed by state-specific guidelines**, as in the case of a crime or death on a property, **or are sensitive enough to warrant a current, local legal opinion about how best to proceed**.*

*In addition, **test questions about a seller being infected with HIV are most likely to make it a nondisclosable condition due to Fair Housing handicapping status**.*

Liability refers to legal responsibility or accountability. ***Upon entering into an agency relationship, agents and principals become subject to a wide range of potential liabilities***, many of which outlive the agency relationship or closing of a particular property transaction.

Licensees and owners who demonstrate ***negligence***, especially ***willful negligence***, in discovering and/or disclosing environmental and material problems that might reasonably be associated with a property may be subject to legal action.

There are ***liability considerations*** for various parties in the event of ***nondisclosure of material defects*** and other property condition issues.

Both the seller and all of the seller's agents, as well as even the buyer's agent, may incur ***legal liability and various penalties*** for nondisclosure and/or nondiscovery depending on a court's determination of fault.

Common ***types of legal liabilities*** include
- ***vicarious***, which refers to a ***supervisor*** or ***principal's responsibility*** for the acts of a ***subordinate*** or ***agent***, respectively; this is most commonly seen in the liability almost any employer has for the professional misdeeds of employees regardless of whether or not they were known to or authorized by the employer
  - *some states, but far from all,* ***have specifically abolished vicarious liability*** *in real estate transactions, especially broker liability for actions of their agents, noting that there is* ***"no imputation of knowledge" on the part of those parties not directly involved with the transaction***
- ***joint***, which means ***shared liability between two or more parties***
- ***several***, which means a ***liability of one party that can be legally pursued separately*** from other liable parties

An agent as well as a principal can incur legal liabilities for such actions as
- ***nondisclosure of property defects*** to a party interested in buying a property
- ***nondisclosure of environmental hazards*** to a party interested in buying a property
- ***nondisclosure of other material information*** to a party interested in buying a property, such as impending major changes to the neighborhood or immediate area

In addition, an agent can incur legal liabilities for such actions as
- ***nondisclosure of agency relationships*** to appropriate parties in a transaction
- ***lack of due diligence or breach of fiduciary duties***

A licensee's statement that "The seller told me the foundation was sound, and I figured, 'Who would know better than the owner?' So I never looked behind the empty packing boxes against the wall in the basement" is hardly a compelling legal defense should the seller actually be trying to conceal foundation problems.

Depending on the claim brought by a party that feels wronged, the state may have a statutory time period, or ***statute of limitations***, *after which the party generally has lost the opportunity to get a legal hearing. Even when a statute of limitations does not apply, a court* may deny a claim based on the concept of **laches**, which means **an unreasonable delay or negligence in bringing a claim in a timely manner**.

***Some questions in this Topic Area are likely to include the word <u>liability</u>, and will be situational,** meaning they will present a scenario **and ask which party or parties are most likely to incur liability** for not discovering, verifying, or disclosing a property condition, or if the property condition requires a disclosure.*

*But look for the word **liability**: it is a good tip that the question is following up on an important point about disclosures and is pointing out that there may be a legally painful consequence for not having made that disclosure at the earliest, or most appropriate, time.*

VI-D. Material Facts Related to Property Condition or Location
(Expect 1-3 questions from this area)

Property conditions that are **material**, which means **significant in a party's decision-making process** of approving or disapproving a purchase, **must, when known or reasonably should have been discovered** by a seller, a seller's agent, or even a buyer's agent, **be disclosed**.

Material facts have to do with discovery and disclosure of any of the elements discussed in the last Topic Area, as well as **any other fact that is significant or essential to a buyer or seller's decision-making process**, even down to the types of available financing and date of closing or possession.

For example, if a buyer needs to move in July 1st but the seller cannot move out until Labor Day, that fact is material to the buyer's final decision and must be shared.

Generally, though, questions about material facts will deal with some of the following common types of **physical or environmental material defects**.

Material defects can include
- **site or soil conditions**, such as being in an area where the water table is too deep for a steady water supply in a dry season, or the topsoil is easily washed away, or the soil is too sandy for grass or gardening
- **property location within a natural hazard zone**, or some other **special study zone** that may affect the property's insurability or insurance rates
  - *As noted in Topic Area II-B, Public Controls Based in Police Power, licensees should ensure that they are aware of whether the property is subject to restrictions due to being in or near a **designated wetland area**, serving as a **habitat for an endangered species**, or **subject to insurance liabilities regardless of FEMA flood insurance rate maps**.*
    - *For example, in the Northeast, many major insurers simply will not write new policies on properties within 2,500 feet of the seacoast as a result of particularly damaging recent storms*
- **undisclosed or undiscovered encroachments or easements**, such as a neighbor's fence that is actually placed within the subject property by three feet
- **structural property environmental problems (internal)**, such as the presence of

- *wood infestation*, such as termites or other wood-boring insects
- *lead-based paint*, which was banned in 1978, so sales contracts for residential properties built *prior to 1978*, are, because of the Residential Lead-Based Paint Hazard Reduction Act of 1992, required to include a federal *disclosure notice; this can be a separate document or a contract component*
- *asbestos*, which was widely used for insulation and causes lung problems
- *radon gas*, which is a colorless, odorless gas that the Surgeon General has warned is the second leading cause of lung cancer, arises from the decay of radioactive minerals in the ground and can collect in a basement or other closed areas
- *urea formaldehyde foam insulation (UFFI)*, which was used extensively in the late 1970's for wall insulation, and may continue to exude formaldehyde gas, is an irritant and potential cancer-causing agent; its use was discontinued in 1980, but its presence in a property must be disclosed
- *toxic mold*, which is becoming an increasingly large problem nationwide
- *structural physical conditions*, such as a leaky roof, outdated wiring or plumbing, foundation cracks, a poorly working water heater or furnace, or some other condition that will become a surprise expense for a new owner, including property alterations or additions that may have been made without permits and could turn into a new owner's problem to reconcile with local zoning authorities.
  - *For example, a property owner in a rural area did not apply for any building permit, but erected a shed that exceeds the allowed size for outbuildings by 10% and is 2' from the property line in a 10' setback zone. Any current owner would have to address local zoning concerns once the nonconforming shed came to their attention, and that potential creates a liability for prospective buyers.*

Licensees should perform the due diligence of identifying the implications of a study zone or other restriction on property ownership, such as whether it requires mandatory flood insurance or zoning approval for property improvements, and then both disclosing and explaining these factors to buyers.

*Licensees and owners who demonstrate **willful negligence** in discovering and/or disclosing any of the above environmental or structural problems that might reasonably be associated with a property may be subject to legal action.*

VI-E. Material Facts Related to Public Controls, Statutes, or Public Utilities
(Expect 1-2 questions from this area)

This Topic Area simply continues the lists from the previous Topic Area, but with a focus on material facts that are other-than site or structural in nature. These include facts related to

- *public controls*, such as discovering and disclosing information on
  - *local zoning and planning* that are currently in effect or may be subject to change
  - *municipal boundaries* that determine school and voting districts as well as availability of public utilities, such as sewer and water, and municipal services, such as waste and recycling pickup, and any special assessments associated with the subject property's specific location

- *property environmental problems (external)*, such as the on-site or nearby presence and effects of
  - *contaminated soil and/or groundwater*, from landfills, chemical discharges, spills, or toxic disposal
  - *underground storage tanks*, which may be deteriorating and/or leaking and contaminating groundwater supplies
  - *commercial, industrial, or utility concerns*, such as airport flight paths, railroad lines. interstate highways, steel or paper mills, nuclear power plants, high-voltage power lines, or cell-phone towers
  - *stigmatized, or psychologically impacted, properties*, such as one in which a crime or murder has been committed; *licensee discovery and disclosure requirements vary across state lines, and will be tested, if at all, on the state-specific portion of the test*
    - *Megan's law is a special area of concern for discovery and disclosure, since it deals with the federally mandated sex offender registry which is governed by state or local authorities; as with other psychologically impacted properties, how licensees conform with Megan's law requirements will be state-specific*

Property defects can be obvious, like sawdust piles that indicate wood boring insects, or they may be more concealed, or *latent*, which means that they are not readily discovered by a normal inspection, and often go undiscovered until after closing.

Latent defects abound, and include such examples as asbestos insulation in a chimney or around enclosed heat ducts, or a cracked foundation that is obscured by dry wall.

A listing *licensee's obligations* include discussing material property conditions with the owner and proceeding according to the legal requirements for the particular conditions.

Remember, *material defects must be disclosed*, and *if an owner instructs a licensee to either remain silent or lie about material defects, the licensee cannot legally obey those instructions*, despite the fiduciary duties of obedience and confidentiality.

If this comes up during a listing presentation, and *if the owner insists*, the licensee would be creating an *invalid contract since it would be based on an illegal purpose*, and so *must decline the listing*.

This ends the presentation of key terms and concepts likely to be either tested or used as distractors in this Content Outline Section.

VII-A. General Knowledge of Contract Law   (Expect 2-4 questions from this area)

This area of real estate relies directly on *basic contract law* for its technical understanding of commonly used *contract terminology*, including common contract *elements*, *provisions*, *contingencies*, and *termination* or *breach* issues.

The following list includes several *opposite pairings* that have specific legal interpretations in understanding the most basic nature of real estate sales contracts, which begins with *whether or not a contract exists*, and if so, *upon which parties it is binding*. For example

- a *valid* contract refers to one that includes *certain critical elements* (these will be itemized below) and so has full legal force and effect
    - an *invalid* contract *lacks at least one of those critical elements*, and is therefore either void or voidable
- a *void* contract is one that has no legal force due to its *lack of one or more elements* required for validity, and can be said to not be a contract at all
    - a *voidable* contract is seen as binding on one party but not on the other, who is free to pursue it or 'void' it
- a *unilateral*, or *'one-sided,'* contract is one in which only one party has made a promise to do something, such as offering a reward to the person who finds a lost pet
    - a *bilateral*, or *'two-sided,'* contract is one in which both parties have made a promise and are obligated to follow through on all of the contract's conditions or risk being in breach of contract
- an *enforceable* contract is one that meets the legal requirements for validity, and therefore is binding on all parties to observe their contractual obligations
    - an *unenforceable* contract may be *either a void contract or one that was valid when made but legally unenforceable* due to some technical fine point, such as the destruction of an unrecorded deed
- an *express* contract generally means that the understanding has been explicitly set out, *typically in writing, though it could be oral*
    - an *implied* contract generally refers to *the conduct of the parties* providing sufficient indication that they have a common understanding

Further, when parties enter into a contract and proceed to satisfy its conditions, the following terms apply

- the term *execute*, as a verb, as in, *"We expect them to execute the contract today,"* can mean <u>*either*</u>
    1. *to sign the contract* or
    2. *to fulfill and complete the contract's conditions*.
        Note: when used in the latter sense, an *executed contract* may also be termed *fully performed*, or *discharged*
- *the term **executory** refers to a contract that is **in the process of being fulfilled***

The specific *basic elements of a valid contract* may vary slightly depending on what kind of contract it is. They may also appear, as is so common in legal language, under interchangeable terms.

Some of the following terms will be further addressed in areas where they have more common applications. However, these elements are commonly identified as

- *legally competent parties*, which means they have *legal capacity* to enter into contracts. This usually *excludes* legal minors and those judged mentally incompetent.
- *offer and acceptance*, also known as a *meeting of the minds*, or *mutual assent*, which means that something is being offered by one party and accepted without qualification by the other
- *consideration*, which means the payment or promise of something of value, generally money, in exchange for what has been offered
- *legal purpose*, or *legality of object*, which means that *the contract is not for an illegal purpose*, such as disposing of toxic waste in an undeveloped residential subdivision, or a house rental in which illegal drugs will be produced
- *reality of consent*, which means that *both parties acted under their own free will*, without *duress*, and that all of the information they had at hand on which to base their decision was accurate and adequate

Other elements that may be required, depending on the contract, include that it

- *be in writing* if required by the *statute of frauds* or other applicable laws for commercial exchanges
  - the *statute of frauds* is a common law statute that has been specifically adopted by many states and requires contracts for the *sale or transfer of interest in real estate* or real estate *rentals for <u>more than</u> one year* to be *in writing in order to be enforceable in court*
- *include all signatures of parties* required to sign, for example, the grantor of a deed
- *give an adequate description of the property* as required for various real estate listing, sales, and mortgage contracts as well as deeds; street addresses may be acceptable for listings and rentals, whereas *an adequate legal description is required for deeds*

A relatively recent federal Act has made certain electronic transmissions legally valid substitutes for hand-written signatures and hard-copy transaction documents. *The Electronic Signatures in Global and National Commerce Act (ESIGN)* (2000) defines and covers the legal force of electronic signatures in *interstate and international commerce*.

ESIGN states that in interstate and foreign commerce, signatures, contracts, and other *transaction documents "may not be denied legal effect, validity, or enforceability solely because [they are] in an electronic form."* It also provides for electronic storage and retention of these records.

Most states have adopted some version of a related model Act, the **Uniform Electronic Transactions Act (UETA)**, *in order to provide state-specific legal definition and validity to electronic records and signatures in business transactions.*

Increasingly, states are conforming with ESIGN standards by noting that the required records may be retained in any format, electronic or otherwise, capable of producing an accurate copy in paper format of the original document.

Breach of contract means a legally unsupportable violation of any of the contract terms by either party and generally gives rise to legal disputes over how to either pursue or abandon the contract. In the event that **contract disputes** arise during the executory period, legal action may follow.

Remedies for a breach include seeking
- **contract rescission**, which basically means cancellation and return of deposits
- **specific performance**, which is **a judicial remedy** that requires getting a court order for the party who breached the contract to honor it
- **monetary damages**, which is another **judicial remedy** that means getting a court-ordered payment of financial restitution
- **liquidated damages**, which is **a nonjudicial remedy** that means getting whatever any **liquidated damages provision, default provision, or forfeiture clause** in the contract stipulates, **such as the forfeiture of earnest money** in the case of buyer default

However, a **liquidated damages** provision in the contract may be written to entitle the seller to keep some or all of the earnest money deposit in the event of a simple **contract cancellation**.

An all-purpose, quick introduction to the "Who's Who" in the legalese of real estate.

Entities, or **parties**, involved in a real estate transaction may be businesses as well as individuals. They take on special names depending on their relationship in a transaction.

Since these terms appear on various transaction-related documents in the normal course of business, **some of them may show up on a test as simple definition questions**.

These and similar terms will be categorized in whatever Content Outline Topic Area is most appropriate for the term and/or the related topic being tested.

The **–er (-or)/-ee** distinction, as in employer/employee, is applied to a variety of pairings in real estate transactions. For here, though, the following are worth noting
- an **offeror** is the party that offers something, an **offeree** is the one to whom it is offered
- a **vendor** is the party that offers something for sale or trade, or actually sells something; a **vendee** is the one that purchases it
- a **mortgagor** is the owner of property that is being put up as collateral for a loan; the **mortgagee** is the one that finances the loan

Most unfamiliar terms that identify parties to a transaction should be pretty easy to figure out on sight if you look at the main word and think through what the –er(-or)/-ee endings mean.

PSI's expanded sub-topic listing includes a few contract-related terms and clauses in this Topic Area that are clustered elsewhere for more logical placement, but will get quick mention here, since it is quite likely that questions based on them will be tallied here
- **assignment**, which means that a person is legally able to transfer their rights in a property
- **novation**, which means substituting one party to a contract for another, thus releasing the first party from further obligation while shifting that obligation to the new party alone; *this was covered as a financing/lender clause in Topic Area IV-D, Mortgages/Deeds of Trust*

- ***acceleration*** *is another clause linked by PSI to this Topic Area; it was covered with other loan-related clauses some pages back in Topic Area IV-D*

VII-B. Listing Agreements   (Expect 1-3 questions from this area)

A ***listing contract***, or ***listing agreement***, is a contract that engages a real estate licensee's firm to market a property in exchange for receiving compensation, usually in the form of a commission, upon the sale and transfer of the property.

A licensee's disclosure and explanation of agency relationships to a principal includes explaining that since a licensee acts as a general agent for a broker, ***when a licensee takes a listing, the licensee is actually creating an agency relationship between the principal and the broker/brokerage firm; the licensee's relationship is as subagent of the broker.***

> *This is the most logical place to note this important point about the creation of agency relationships; however, questions about a licensee's disclosure and explanation may be tallied in Topic Area V-B, Creation and Disclosure of Agency.*

> *Also, in a close, legal interpretation of agency relationships, it can be argued that because the agency relationship created by listing contracts is between the principal and the licensee's broker/brokerage firm,* ***the listing licensee*** *is not a fiduciary for the principal—that's the position of the broker/brokerage firm—but* ***does owe fiduciary duties to the principal on behalf of the broker/brokerage firm.***

> *These distinctions are legally too refined for testing, but are mentioned here to help address the finer distinctions that are commonly left unexplained in textbooks. They may also help you understand* ***the basic legal right brokerages have for retaining listings when listing licensees leave the firm***, *or even the authority to transfer listings to another agent, such as if the principal becomes dissatisfied with the listing licensee.*

Listing agreement contracts, like all contracts, ***require some very specific elements*** for their legal validity. In addition, though, they may contain a host of other components that address common practice, terms, and conventions in a particular market area or state.

The following elements need to be added to the basic elements necessary for a valid contract as detailed in Topic Area VII-A, General Knowledge of Contract Law, to create a valid listing agreement
- ***required signatures***, which include ***all*** of the owners ***and*** the listing licensee
- ***property description*** sufficient to identify the property; it need not be the legal description required on a deed and is often just the street address
- ***list price*** of the property
- ***definite termination date***, which ensures that a property owner does not get locked into an arrangement that the owner has to actively terminate
- ***broker compensation***, which describes when it is earned and how it is computed

The above elements are often reinforced by state regulations and tested in state-specific detail, where applicable, on the state portion of the exam. In most states, there are also ***property*** *disclosures* as required by state law along with other elements, such as a definite starting date, prohibitions on automatic renewal clauses, and others.

Also, this area *may* contain questions similar to those in V-C, Responsibilities of Agent, on such *points about listing agreements* as the following

- *the seller* is *the final authority with responsibility for establishing a list price*, not the licensee preparing a CMA or an appraiser who has performed an appraisal
- *a listing agreement is an employment contract* that grants a licensee the authority for seller representation

The most common types of listing agreements are

- *exclusive right to sell*, which engages a single licensee to market the property and entitles that licensee to a commission regardless of who finds the buyer, even if it is the property owner; *this provides the greatest protection for the licensee to collect compensation*
- *exclusive agency*, which engages a single licensee to market the property and entitles that licensee to a commission if anyone **other than** the property owner finds the buyer; if the owner finds the buyer, the licensee gets no commission
- *open*, or *nonexclusive*, which allows the property owner to engage any number of licensees to market the property, and only entitles the licensee who procures the buyer to a commission; if the property owner finds the buyer, none of the licensees are entitled to any compensation
- *net*, which engages a licensee to market a property and receive as compensation all sale proceeds in excess of the owner's stated "net" for the property

  > *Note: net listings are illegal in many states and are widely viewed as unethical due to their potential for creating a licensee **conflict of interest**, or even direct exploitation of an unsophisticated seller. But they are defined here, and tested, because they represent a way of structuring a listing agreement and compensation, regardless of local rulings on their legality.*

VII-C. Buyer/Tenant Representation Agreements, including Key Elements and Provisions of Buyer and/or Tenant Agreements (Expect 1-2 questions from this area)

A *buyer-broker agreement*, *buyer agency agreement*, or *agency employment contact*, is a contract that engages a real estate licensee to search for suitable property on behalf of a potential buyer in exchange for receiving compensation, usually in the form of a commission, upon the purchase and transfer of the property. *Tenant may be substituted for buyer whenever appropriate for the situation under consideration, since agency relationship between a licensee and either type of consumer observes the same set of fiduciary duties and disclosures.*

In these arrangements the licensee is often referred to as a *buyer's broker* when representing only the buyer.

The most common types of *buyer agency agreements* are

- *exclusive buyer agency*, which engages a single licensee to search for a suitable property and entitles that licensee to compensation regardless of who finds the property, even if it is the buyer – its listing agreement counterpart is the exclusive right-to-sell listing

- ***exclusive-agency buyer agency***, which engages a single licensee to search for a suitable property and entitles that licensee to a compensation if anyone other than the buyer finds a suitable property – its listing agreement counterpart is the exclusive agency listing
- ***open buyer agency***, or ***nonexclusive***, which allows the buyer to engage any number of licensees to search for a suitable property, and only entitles the licensee who introduces the buyer to the purchased property to compensation; if the buyer finds the property, none of the licensees are entitled to any compensation – its listing agreement counterpart is the open listing

Note: The above distinctions are gaining widespread recognition and even some state-specific acceptance, statutory definition, and use; they are presented here more for informational purposes than for testing.

*However, read **all** questions regarding types of buyer brokerage very carefully – **the concepts and some terms are gaining sufficient national use to warrant appearing on the test as scored questions** instead of simple distractors.*

*Questions on buyer agency will be very similar to those on listings, but the emphasis will be on an agent's **duties as a buyer's agent** rather than a seller's agent, which are the same, just on the opposite side of the transaction.*

These questions may also present examples of licensee and agent conduct, identifying their obligations to disclose agency relationships to other parties in real estate transactions as well as explain different types of agency relationship, such as single or dual agency. If so, they will probably be tallied in Topic Area V-B, Creation and Disclosure of Agency.

VII-D. Offers/Purchase Agreements (Expect 2-4 questions from this area)

The paperwork and documentation trail in a real estate sales transaction proceeds from listing a property to ***offers***, ***counteroffers***, and ***sales contracts***.

Offers, like so many other real estate terms, may have a locally 'correct' label, such as ***offer to purchase***, ***offer to purchase and contract***, and similar terms. The purpose of an offer is ***to set forth the conditions the prospective buyer proposes to the seller.***

But ***an offer is not a contract***, since the offeree has not accepted it; ***it may, though, become a binding contract upon acceptance of all of its conditions by the offeree***.

A ***counteroffer*** is the common term for the offer ***if the offeree*** makes ***a change of any kind to it and returns it to the original offeror*** (see the next Topic Area for more)

Earnest money is the term for the deposit, or down payment, that ***accompanies an offer*** to purchase real estate; it serves to demonstrate the buyer's good-faith, "earnest" intention to complete the transaction and supply the full purchase price, or consideration, at closing.

If the contract includes a ***liquidated damages provision***, earnest money may also provide a source of funds ***for damages to the seller in the event of buyer default***.

Both the use and the amount of earnest money are governed more by convention than law; *earnest money does not constitute "consideration" and is not a legal requirement for creating a binding sales contract*. However, most offers are accompanied by *some* earnest money, and *a buyer's seriousness of purpose* is commonly seen in direct proportion to the size of the earnest money check.

These and other critical earnest money considerations, such as *how much a buyer provides*, *conditions of its use and/or return* in the event of offer rejection or sales contract termination, and *liquidated damages provisions* are *all subject to negotiation between the parties*.

Once an offer or counteroffer has become a mutually accepted and binding contract, it is variously known as a *purchase agreement*, a *purchase contract*, a *sales contract*, a *purchase and sale contract*, an *agreement for sale*, or another similar term.

A properly executed purchase agreement identifies the specific property, sets out all of the contractual requirements for its transfer from one party to another, and generally serves as the complete agreement between parties.

As previously noted, *offer and acceptance* is a requirement of a valid contract, and is generally the final element needed for creating a valid real estate purchase agreement.

In some states, such as North Carolina, acceptance must be paired with notification to the offeror in order to achieve fully defensible and binding legal effect; notification is a prudent protection for an offeree in any jurisdiction and can help defend the priority of an accepted offer in a multiple-submission situation.

Precisely what constitutes binding notification—oral, written, certified, and/or some electronic means—varies by jurisdiction, so check with a real estate attorney in the subject property's state to ensure you have "closed the loop."

Once all of the contract details have been negotiated and there is a binding contract, each party acquires certain *contractual rights and responsibilities*. Some of these include
- *equitable title*, which means that the buyer, during the executory period of contract fulfillment, has a property interest, specifically *the right to acquire formal legal title*, which in turn *may allow the buyer to transfer or assign that right*
- *assignment*, which means that the buyer may transfer their rights in a property

Contract *provisions* refer to the particular information, conditions, and instructions provided in the contract that govern the many details that have to be addressed in *the 'performance'* of the contract.

Provisions are too numerous to list, or test, in detail, but include commonplace elements like
- *personal property included*, which specifies what stays, like firewood or appliances
  (*Ownership of personal property* is legally transferred at closing through a *bill of sale*, which will trump all other options in a test question on this point.)

- *time is of the essence clause*, which serves to underline and *reinforce the importance of meeting contract dates*, and that *failure to do so will be considered a contract breach and grounds for cancellation of the contract*
- *rescission clause*, which allows one of the parties, generally through a contract-specific contingency or regulated-sale review period, to *rescind*, or *cancel* the contract without penalty. Rescind refers *to "unmaking" a contract* and *restoring the parties to their precontractual position, including the return of all monies*
- *option*, which is most often in *commercial property purchase offers* and serves to hold an offer open for a specified period *in exchange for some monetary consideration*, which is *generally (1) applied toward the purchase price* if all of the conditions are met and the sale goes through, *or (2) kept by the owner if there is no sale*
    - an *option is a unilateral contract*, which is *binding on the seller to sell, but not on the buyer to buy*
- *"as is"* refers to the property being sold in its existing condition without guarantees for its physical condition or title; *this provision generally does not protect a seller from liability for known material defects*
- *"subject to" a mortgage*, which refers to a seller retaining the mortgage and the liability for payments, but the new owner would pay the mortgage payments
- *liquidated damages*, which refers to a clause specifying particular amounts due to an aggrieved party in the event of breach or default, such as a seller keeping earnest money
    - *default provisions* in some states may include a *forfeiture clause*, which specifies how much (generally all) of an earnest money deposit may be kept by a seller in the event of buyer default on a binding contract
- *settlement or closing instructions*, which detail who pays for what, such as tax prorations, property repairs, title insurance, and other transaction expenses

A contract *contingency* is a *special condition* or provision inserted by either party that must be met in order for an approved offer to become a fully binding contract. *In the event the contingency is not satisfied, the contract is considered void.* *(In practice, disputes may arise.)*

Common contingencies include
- *financing*, which typically asserts that the contract is contingent on the buyer's being approved for a certain type of loan by a particular date
- *property sale*, which typically asserts that a buyer's current property must be sold prior to the target closing date for the new property
- *property inspection*, which typically asserts that a professional home inspection report must show that the true condition of the property is acceptable to the buyer

VII-E. Counteroffers/Multiple Counteroffers   (Expect 1-2 questions from this area)

As previously noted, a *counteroffer* is the common term for the offer *if the offeree* makes *a change of any kind to it and returns it to the original offeror*. The following principles apply to offers and counteroffers
- *any change* to the original offer legally *terminates that offer* and indicates the original has been *rejected and replaced* by the updated offer; the same is true of a counteroffer
- *changes to offers and counteroffers should be initialed by all principals*

- an *offer*, or *counteroffer*, can be *revoked by the offeror* at any time prior to its acceptance
- the *offeree may cancel* the offer simply *by letting the response period expire without responding*

Submission of offers and counteroffers is commonly understood to mean that an agent is responsible for *submitting all offers*, regardless of the terms offered or whether the property is already under contract.

Further, even when the principal has instructed the agent not to present offers of a certain type or from certain parties, the agent is commonly expected to inform the principal of all offers.

> *Some of the questions in this area will be scenario-type that serve to illustrate the above point of **submitting all offers**, not just the best, or those over a particular amount, or with certain conditions, but **all offers**.*

> *Other aspects of submitting offers, such as requirements to make e-mail correspondence, fax transmissions, or oral binders legally binding, are subject to local interpretations, so are unlikely to be tested on the general exam. Where there are state regulations on these matters, there may be questions on the state-specific portion of the exam.*

A variety of other events can *terminate offers and counteroffers*, many of which are examples of conditions that arise *by operation of law*, which means that existing laws make them happen automatically, without any direct action or intent of a party. A few events that may terminate an offer or counteroffer include the

- *death* of a party to the contract, which automatically voids an offer or counteroffer, since there has been no completed *offer and acceptance*
- *bankruptcy* of a one of the parties

VII-F. Leases   (Expect 1-3 questions from this area)

As noted in Topic Area I-D, Types of Ownership, *estates in real property* are divided into *freehold estates* and *nonfreehold estates*, or *less-than-freehold estates; nonfreehold estates* are commonly referred to as *leasehold estates*.

> *Leasehold estates are contracts*, and *are classified as personal property, not real property*. Therefore, whereas they typically entitle the lessee to all of the possession-and-use rights of ownership, *they do not entitle the lessee to transfer title, encumber it with liens, or make alterations to the property* without the knowledge and consent of the owner.

> > Since leases are contracts, the *sale or other transfer of rental property* ownership during a lease period *typically has no effect on existing leases* – new owners must honor the terms of all leases.

> > *Exceptions* to this include *some foreclosure sales* and *most eminent domain condemnations*, which may cancel existing leases and other property use agreements.

Common *elements of a valid lease* include many of the same elements for other real estate contracts, such as a *description of the property*, that the lease must be for a *legal use of the property*, *mutual agreement*, *legal capacity of parties*, and *required signatures*.

In addition, the *statute of frauds* requires leases for *over a year to be in writing*; this means that *oral leases for one year or less are legally valid and binding*.

However, *an unwritten lease is subject to dispute* about who really promised what, so does not protect either party as well as a written agreement.

A *lease purchase* is *typically a rent-to-own arrangement* where an agreed-upon portion of the rent is applied toward the purchase price and either when the tenant can arrange other financing or when the full price is paid, ownership transfers

Types of leases, leasehold estates, and lease clauses and provisions were covered in previous PSI outlines in a separate Topic Area: Property Management and Landlord/Tenant.

These lease and property management topics include over 20 terms that are covered in most full-scope prelicensing texts, and part of even an entry-level real estate professional's vocabulary.

SPECIAL EXAM NOTE: Just because PSI removed the Topic Area does NOT mean that it deleted all—or any—of the questions based on these terms; rather, PSI could easily reassign them to THIS or some other related Topic Area.

SPECIAL SPECIAL EXAM-PREP NOTE*: The next four pages consolidates a lot of important lease and management agreement information, but there is no room on the exam to test on more than one, two, or, at MOST, three points. So skimming over it probably won't seriously hurt your chances of passing the test, especially if you are strong on all the other Contract Topics.*

Regardless, to be a well-informed professional, you would do well to read carefully through the following material to become familiar with the most common of them, especially since a few definitions below may get tested and tallied in this—or even another—Topic Area.

Property management topics begin here with a look at types of leasehold estates.

Note for the following description of types of leasehold estates: these names appear in textbooks using the terms "estate" and "tenancy" interchangeably, as in "estate for years" and "tenancy for years," the convention here, as in both common practice and test questions, will be to use "tenancy."

Common types of leasehold estates include
- *tenancy for years*, which means that there is *a definite termination date*. *Vacation rentals* as well as *commercial leases* are often written this way, and may run for whatever time period suits both parties, such as Memorial Day through Labor Day for the former, or a few days for storage to many years for an industrial site for the latter. An important characteristic of these leases is that *no notice is required for termination*, at which time the old tenant simply has to be out to make way for whatever new use or tenants the landlord has for the property.

However, some contracts may have *an option to renew with a deadline for exercising that option*.

- *tenancy from period to period*, or *periodic tenancy*, which means there is *no definite termination date, just recurring time periods (e.g., year-to-year or month-to-month)* during which one party or the other may exercise an option to terminate it. This is a *common tenancy arrangement in residential leases,* which may include an automatic renewal, or 'evergreen' clause, that allows the lease to automatically renew for the same period and general terms unless one of the parties cancels the renewal by providing proper notice to terminate.

- *tenancy at will*, which is *similar to a tenancy from period to period except that there is no specified periodic nature* to it – it is simply at the will and discretion of the landlord and may be terminated at almost any time by either party. These situations may include an owner letting a tenant remain in a property being taken by eminent domain right up to the last minute, or tenants being given the option to move out whenever a job transfer or alternate housing situation arises.

- *tenancy at sufferance*, which means that a tenant has *refused to vacate* at the end of a tenancy for years or periodic tenancy and *remains in possession of the property against the will of the landlord*. Generally, a landlord will not accept or cash rent checks to avoid appearing to approve the tenant's continuation.
    - *holdover tenant* is the term used to describe a tenant who remains against the landlord's will in a tenancy at sufferance.

The names of various *common lease types* suggest the financial structure of the revenues, or *method of payment*. Some of these include

- *gross lease*, or *straight lease*, which means the *tenant pays a flat fee out of which the owner pays all standard property expenses*, such as taxes, association fees, and, in some cases, utilities. *Most residential leases are gross leases*.

- *net lease*, under which the *tenant pays a base rent and some or all of the property expenses*, beginning with utilities, taxes, and special assessments; *some appraisal authorities consider this term synonymous with net-net and net-net-net leases*
    - *net-net leases are negotiated to require additional tenant obligations, typically insurance – these are not very common in current practice*
    - *net-net-net leases*, or *triple-net leases*, are generally negotiated to make the *tenant responsible for paying all expenses*, including maintenance, repairs, and in some cases, the owner's mortgage interest
        - *absolute net lease*, cover extensive expenses according to contract negotiations, as well as typically making the tenant responsible for structural maintenance

- *full-service lease* is a lease in which *the landlord agrees to pay all maintenance, property taxes, and insurance*

- *percentage leases* have a *fixed base rental fee plus a percentage of the gross or net income in excess of a predetermined minimum sales volume*; these are *common in retail properties*

- *graduated leases*, which establish a *schedule for rent increases, generally based on a business tenant's anticipated growth* of gross or net income

- *index leases* are *similar to graduated leases, but the rental amounts may go up or down, generally in reference to the consumer price index* or the *cost-of-living index*

- *lease purchase*, which is *typically a rent-to-own arrangement* where an agreed-upon portion of the rent is applied toward the purchase price and either when the tenant can arrange other financing or when the full price is paid, ownership transfers
- *lease-option*, or *lease with an option to buy*, is a mixture of a lease and a purchase contract, but begins as *a lease with a clause allowing the tenant to exercise an option to purchase the property*

Some other types of leases refer to the *property type* rather than payment type. Examples of these include

- *ground lease*, or *land lease*, generally is *a long-term commercial or industrial lease of land only, with the tenant typically erecting a building* that reverts to the landowner at the end of the rental period, which may be as long as 99 years. *Ground leases are commonly structured and paid as some form of net lease.*
- *oil-and-gas lease*, which grants the right to extract oil and gas from a specified property, usually in exchange for *an up-front fee and royalties* from any oil or gas produced

Common *lease provisions and clauses* include

- *covenant of quiet enjoyment*, which entitles the tenant to *undisturbed possession and use of the property*. Most leases qualify this right to allow the landlord to enter the premises periodically during business hours for maintenance and inspections, as well as for emergencies.
- *term of lease provision*, which generally *gives the start and end dates, may also, in the case of a periodic residential lease, include an automatic renewal provision*, or *evergreen clause*, which extends the lease unless one of the parties specifically terminates it according to the process indicated in the provision
- *escalator clause*, or *escalation clause*, or *step-up clause*, which *specifies the terms and conditions of rent increases*; they are central to graduated leases, though they can be found in any lease
- *right of first refusal* clause may be included in a lease when the tenant wants the opportunity to purchase the property in the event the owner decides to sell; *it gives the tenant the right to review any sales offer the owner receives and either match it or else let the owner proceed with a sale to a different party*
- *subletting*, or *subleasing*, which refers to a *tenant leasing the property to someone else*. When not prohibited, *the original tenant remains primarily liable to the landlord for rents and property condition*.
- *assignment* refers to a tenant *transferring the lease and some or all of its liability to another person*. In some cases, the landlord or the lease will allow the complete substitution of the original tenant by the new tenant regarding lease responsibilities and let the new tenant assume sole, primary responsibility for the rest of the lease period.

Owned and leased inclusions represent an especially important provision in commercial leases to ensure clear mutual understandings about whether *tenant improvements* are owner or tenant owned and/or reimbursable.

Fixtures, mentioned in Content Area I, are of special importance in leased property. Generally, anything a residential tenant *attaches* to a rental unit in a permanent manner can be argued as becoming real property and thus must be left in the unit at the end of the lease period.

Separation and removal, regardless of whether it is approved by both parties, is known as ***severance*** and ***turns whatever was severed from the real property into personal property***.

Trade fixtures are more commonly understood to remain the tenant's property, though all tenant-provided ***improvements***, both residential and commercial, should be spelled out as ***owned or leased inclusions*** to avoid confusion.

Reversionary rights in property management generally refer to ***the reinstatement of the owner's full ownership and possession rights at the end of the lease period***

The term for the ***transfer of ownership of improvements*** is ***accession***, and is often part of an owner's ***reversionary right***.

> *This is of particular importance in many long-term commercial and industrial leases, since lease terms often make tenant improvements, including buildings and facilities, the landowner's property at the end of the term.*

Abandonment refers to a tenant's ***vacating a rental property prior to the end of the lease term and defaulting on the rent***. A few terms related to the property of a tenant in default is
- ***distrain***, ***distraint***, or ***distress***, which refer to the right of a landlord, generally after a court order, to seize a tenant's personal property for rent in arrears

> *Some states have specific time periods and legal language to clarify what constitutes **legal abandonment** and a landlord's rights to enter and regain possession of the property, as well as the tenant's continued financial liability. Where applicable, these may be part of the state-specific portion of the test.*

Evictions may be ***initiated by either the landlord or the tenant***. Although they are handled according to state-specific procedures, they are commonly referred to by the same terms
- ***actual eviction*** is the ***landlord's recourse*** when a tenant has breached the lease, such as nonpayment of rent or exceeding the occupancy limit. This is typically effected by the landlord's bringing a ***suit for possession*** in court; *the legal details and timing vary from place to place.*
- ***constructive eviction*** is the ***tenant's recourse*** when the landlord has breached the lease by ***letting the property become uninhabitable through conscious neglect***. This kind of neglect on the part of the landlord ***relieves the tenant from the obligation to pay rent***. *Again, though, the **details of the process may vary from place to place**.*

A ***property management contract*** defines the relationship between a property manager and an owner. Through the contract, the owner typically authorizes the ***property manager to act as a general agent***, able to make a wide range of binding decisions in the course of managing the property. These activities include, but are not limited to, the authority to
- ***select tenants***
- ***prepare and sign leases***
- ***collect and deposit rents***
- ***hire and pay employees***

- *contract* with maintenance and repair contractors
- *make risk management decisions*, such as selecting insurance coverages
- *prepare operating budgets*
- *determine gross effective income*
- *maintain office accounts*
- *monitor and pay fixed operating expenses* such as salaries and taxes
- *establish a reserve account* for variable expenses, such as repairs and supplies

The property management agreement itself generally includes the following *key elements*
- *property description*
- *contract period and termination provisions*
- *property management's duties, scope of authority, and limitations*
- *statement of the owner's purpose or objective*, such as maximizing income or increasing property value: *trying to achieve the owner's objective is generally considered to be the primary duty of a property manager*
- *statement of the owner's obligations and duties*
- *frequency and types of reporting to the owner*
- *management compensation arrangements*, which are generally based on a percentage of gross income. However, rates for property management services *are established by negotiation between the principal and the property manager*

Rental related discriminatory laws include many federal laws presented above for property sales, but with direct application to property management processes and particulars.

Special Note: much of the following, especially the federal laws, is adapted from previous material to reinforce their direct application to property management processes and particulars.

In the course of renting properties, the landlord or owner has to pay attention to many of the same *federal Fair Housing, lending, and credit laws* that govern property sales, plus some *handicapped access requirements* and *property condition disclosures.*

Federal Fair Housing laws provide *protection against discrimination in the <u>rental</u>, or <u>advertising</u> of residential property* for *protected classes* based on the same personal characteristics identified in Topic Area IX-B regarding property sales.

Protected classes under Fair Housing laws include *race or color, national origin, religious preference, sex, handicapping conditions,* and/or *familial status*.

As a reminder here, the particulars of handicapping conditions and familial status will be repeated to both reinforce their details and save you from having to flip back to IX-B.
- *handicapping condition*, which means having a physical or mental disability, including infection with the HIV virus or recovery status for drug and alcohol dependence, that substantially limits one or more major life activity
- *familial status*, which means *one or more individuals under 18 years of age being domiciled* with a parent or custodian, or the legal designee of the parents, and also

applies to any person who is pregnant or in the process of securing legal custody of any individual under 18 years old

- *an age exemption* to familial status protection for multi-unit properties *may apply* to housing that is
  - intended for and *solely occupied by* persons *62 years of age or older*
  - intended primarily for *"55 and over,"* meaning *80 percent or more of the units* are occupied by *at least one occupant 55 years of age or older*

Important Fair Housing reminder for property management: In residential property rentals covered by Fair Housing requirements, a *landlord must allow a handicapped tenant to make reasonable modifications to a unit at the tenant's own expense*, typically *with the obligation to return the unit to its previous condition when moving out.*

Special clarification/reminder: This requirement is based on Fair Housing laws, NOT the Americans With Disabilities Act (ADA) requirements, which apply to public accessibility.

Also, just as in property sales, licensees and unlicensed property managers alike must avoid the following *discriminatory practices in marketing and tenant selection* that are *violations of Fair Housing laws*

- *steering*, which means showing prospective renters of a particular protected class properties only in areas that have a high representation of the same protected class
- *blockbusting*, which means 'spreading the word' that the neighborhood may be about to decline in safety and quality of life factors due to an increased presence in the area of a particular protected class, so *tenants should consider relocating*

Equal Credit Opportunities Act (ECOA), which applies when a property manager is reviewing an applicant's credit and employment history – *the property manager is required to ignore the following factors about an applicant when reviewing a credit application*

- *race or color*
- *religion or national origin*
- *sex or marital status*
- *age (over the age of majority)*
- *receipt of income from public assistance programs, such as food stamps*
- *a good faith exercise of any right under the Consumer Credit Protection Act*

Lead-Based Paint Hazard Reduction Act, which applies to both the sale and rental of *residential properties built before 1978*, and requires landlords to provide tenants of units covered by the Act as well as all rental applicants with a *standard disclosure pamphlet* and also *to attach a disclosure form to new leases, unless the disclosure information is included in the text of the lease*

VII-G. Other Real Estate Contracts   (Expect 0-2 questions from this area)

The term *option* commonly refers to either an *option to purchase, an option clause most commonly seen in commercial property purchase offers*, or a *lease-option*; options are similar to, yet quite different from, a *right of first refusal* arrangement.

An *option* in a *commercial property purchase offer* serves to hold an offer open for a specified period *in exchange for some monetary consideration*, which is *generally*
(1) applied toward the purchase price if all of the conditions are met and the sale goes through, *or*
(2) simply kept by the owner if there is no sale.

- an *option is a unilateral contract*, which is *binding on the seller to sell, but not on the buyer to buy*

A *lease-option*, or *lease with an option to buy*, is a mixture of a lease and a purchase contract, but begins as a lease with *a clause allowing the tenant to exercise an option to purchase the property*.

The information on lease-options is presented here for comparison with option contracts for purchases; lease-options will most likely be tallied for testing in the previous Topic Area.

A *right of first refusal (ROFR* or *RFR)* is a contractual agreement giving the holder the option to either purchase or pass on a property before the owner sells it to another party. Since it is a contractual right, *it is subject to negotiation of both specific conditions and financial consideration for the grantor.*

In some common interest ownership properties, especially condos and coops, the owners association may retain an RFR on individual units; they are also often included in some business partnerships or multiple-private-owner arrangements to avoid partition sales or transfers that could potentially damage the remaining owners.

Often, though, RFRs are simply oral understandings between parties, such as family members saying they will give certain other family members first refusal on a particular property or family object with sentimental value.

An *RFR* clause may be included in a lease when the tenant wants the opportunity to purchase the property in the event the owner decides to sell; *it gives the tenant the right to review any sales offer the owner receives and either match it or else let the owner proceed with a sale to a different party.*

This ends the presentation of key terms and concepts likely to be either tested or used as distractors in this Content Outline Section.

VIII-A. Title Insurance   (Expect 1-2 questions from this area)

Regardless of which type of deed is used to convey and warrant title, there may be a *defect in the title*, or something that might put a *cloud on the title*, meaning that there are conflicting claims that prevent the absolute legal conveyance of *clear title*.

Title insurance is a common way to address the risk of buying a property with *existing, undiscovered title defects*, since title insurance *insures the policyholder against the <u>future discovery</u> of <u>certain past problems</u>*.

Common defects include *forged documents* or *undisclosed third-party interests*, such as a *lis pendens*, which is Latin for "a pending lawsuit," *liens*, *undiscovered ownership interests* of spouses or family members, and *unrecorded prior transfers or assignments*.

A professional *title search* generally discovers all of the recorded information about the property's *liens*, *lis pendens*, and sometimes the *chain of title* back *to the original owner*; most title searches look back to a recorded land transaction far enough in the past to be recognized by statutory requirements as *the root of title*, or starting point, to demonstrate clear title.

> *By definition, a **chain of title is the ownership history back to the original owner**, who may have received title through a **charter** or **land grant** from the King of England, ruler of France or Spain, or a **warrant** or **patent** from the state or federal government, or even a **charter or contract** from a colonial-era tribal leader or **New England sachem**, depending on the state.*

>> *However, local convention as well as statutory provisions in many states only requires searching the past 40-60 years to identify a **root of title** for an unbroken chain of ownership in a **due-diligence confirmation of marketable title**.*

>> *In some states, attorneys handle title searches and prepare an **attorney's opinion of title**, whereas in others the name for the most thorough type of search, which summarizes all documents in all official sources, is an **abstract of title**, and is performed by an **abstractor**.*

If the search identifies a *cloud on the title*, it may be resolved through a *quiet title action* or *quiet title suit*, or *suit to quiet title*, which is a court pleading that leads to a judge's decision on the matter. Or the cloud may also be lifted, and the need for a quiet title action removed, by *getting a quitclaim deed* from the newly discovered party with a real, or potential, interest in the property.

Title insurance policies are commonly classified as *standard coverage policies* and *extended coverage policies*, and though the extended coverage insures against more risks, such as unrecorded mechanics liens or undisclosed survey and zoning problems, standard coverage policies typically include common basic coverages such as problems arising from

- *forged documents*
- *unknown or undisclosed heirs*
- *hidden incompetency of grantors*
- *public record errors*, such as misfiled documents
- *incorrect marital statements*

When a *title insurance company* performs a title search, it generally prepares what is commonly known as a *title report*, or *preliminary title report*, or *certificate of title*, that shows whether the title is clear and insurable.

If it is, the company will provide a *commitment for title insurance*, or *title commitment*, or *binder*, which is *the policy offer, explanation of coverages, and commitment to insure*.

The two most common types of policies are

- *owner's policy*, which covers the new property owner for the purchase price of the property; it remains in effect even beyond the new owner's selling the property later on *and may be paid for by either party, depending on the sales contract and/or local convention*

- *lender's policy*, or *mortgagee's policy*, or *loan policy*, which covers the lender for the remaining loan balance at the time of a claim; these policies expire as soon as the loan is fully repaid *and are typically paid for by the borrower*

*In the event a claim has to be paid to buy out a legitimate, undisclosed interest, the title insurance company exercises its right of **subrogation**. This means, roughly, that since they have made the payment to, or on behalf of, the insured, the company is entitled to recover its costs by suing for and keeping damages from any wrongdoers or other liable parties.*

*Note: the term above, **subrogation**, is not appropriate for real estate testing since it is specific to insurance processes; it is mentioned here both for informational purposes and because it may be used as a distractor, especially in questions about **subordination provisions** in loans.*

Title insurance *premiums* are typically made in a *single payment, due at closing*.

VIII-B. Deeds
(Expect 1-2 questions from this area)

A *deed* is *a written instrument by which land is conveyed*. There are several areas of note about deeds: terminology, elements of validity, common types of deeds, covenants and warranties, and title issues.

The *terminology* for parties to a deed includes knowing that the one who is *granting*, or giving away, ownership is referred to as the *grantor*, and the new owner is known as the *grantee*.

There are some *legal elements of validity* that are required in order for a deed to be legally *valid* and *enforceable*. While some states require a few more than others, most require, at a minimum, the following elements or conditions

- it must be *in writing*
- the grantor must have *legal capacity*, that is, be of legal age and mental competence
- *identification of the parties*, that is, the grantor and the grantee must be named
- *statement of consideration*, or what is being paid/exchanged for the property. While this is often expressed as a nominal sum, as in "for $10 and other good and valuable consideration," increasingly it is the actual sales price
- *words of conveyance*, or a *granting clause*, such as, "I do hereby grant and convey"
- *a legal description of the property*
- *signature of the grantor*

- *delivery* and *acceptance (or **registration** when using the **Torrens system** in those 10 states that recognize it)*

In some states, there are additional requirements, such as

- an *habendum clause*, which defines the extent and limitations of the interest conveyed; it generally begins with the words "to have and to hold," and so is often referred to as the *"to-have-and-to-hold" clause.* Sometimes it is considered part of the granting clause.
- a *seal*, or mark of authentication. It is often just the printed, or written, word "Seal" or the initials "L.S." (for the Latin term meaning "the place of the seal") by the line for the grantor's signature.

Other common parts and processes of deed creation may include

- the *date*
- *relevant exceptions and restrictions*
- *acknowledgement*, or formal statement that the grantor is the one signing the deed and is doing so voluntarily
- *recording* the deed in the public records to provide notice of its existence
  - *public records may be housed and maintained by the municipality itself or centralized in either a county or state location, depending on the type of document (birth, marriage, and death certificates; divorce decrees; probate records; etc.) as well as the state: **the county system is used widely, but not exclusively, nationwide for land records.***

Recording a document provides what is referred to as *constructive notice*, or *legal notice*, which means that a *due diligence* review of the public record would make the existence of the document known to the reviewer. This differs from *actual notice*, which means that a party *has personally received the notice*, as when a process server delivers a subpoena to appear in court.

Recording the deed provides *constructive notice that title has been transferred* to the new owner.

This is critically important in protecting an owner's title interest, since *proper, legal recording establishes a new owner's position and rights within the chain of title*.

The specific process for recording deeds and other documents *may* involve formal *acknowledgments* of signatures by witnesses and/or *notarization* in order to create a legally valid recordation; *the process details for recording documents are state-specific and therefore not testable on this section of the test*.

Types of deeds are as varied as the purposes they serve and the covenants and warranties they include. Some of the more common ones are

- *general warranty deeds*, or *warranty deeds*, which *include all of the five covenants listed below*, and *offer the greatest protection for the grantee of all deeds*
- *special warranty deeds*, which warrant the *title against title defects that arose <u>only</u> during the grantor's ownership*

- *bargain and sale deeds*, which contain *no guaranty from the grantor about the validity of title, but implies that the grantor has an interest* that is being sold to the grantee
- *quitclaim deeds*, which have *no covenants or warranties*. They simply relinquish any and all interest the grantor may have in a property. They are commonly used to ensure that a particular party will not decide to interfere later; *they provide the least protection for the grantee* against other potential problems with the title.

The following *additional types of deeds* are less common than those above but do appear in various national textbooks. *Some are state-specific or go by different names in different jurisdictions, so are not fair game for testing, except as distractors, on this part of the test*. They include

- *grant deeds*, *which are used in a few states, notably in the West, in place of a general warranty deed, which contains additional warranties*
- *tax deeds*, *which transfer ownership after a tax sale*
- *sheriff's deeds*, *which transfer property for certain forced or judicial sales*
- *correction deeds*, *which simply correct errors or omissions in a previous deed*
- *confirmatory deeds*, *which is often the same as a correction deed, but in some states is used to affirm title based on a final order in a suit to quiet title*
- *gift deeds*, *which are deeds given for either a nominal sum or "love and affection"*
- *mortgage deeds*, *which are deeds used in some states, whereby a property owner borrowing money secured by the property gives a lender, who is sometimes the seller using this deed for seller-financing, **legal title and specific contractual rights** to claim and/or sell the property if the borrower is in breach of loan provisions*
- *executor's deeds*, *or **administrator's deeds**, which are used in some states to convey property of those who died with or without a will, respectively*
  - *certificate of devise, descent, or distribution or some other state-specific form may be used by a probate judge to convey willed and family-retained properties*

*Special note: Since **trust deeds**, or **deeds of trust**, are mortgage financing instruments, the term(s) would only appear in this Topic Area as a distractor.*

Deeds may include a variety of *covenants and warranties*. Covenants are *formal agreements or promises*; warranties are *guarantees*. The *five most common* are the

- *covenant of seisin*, which means the grantor claims to be the owner of the property and is therefore legally entitled to convey it; *seisin is a Middle English/Old French word for "possession," and is related to—and pronounced like—the word "seize"*
- *covenant of quiet enjoyment*, which means the grantor promises that no one will disturb the new owner with claims against the property, such as an undisclosed co-owner or a long-lost heir
- *covenant of further assurance*, which means the grantor assumes responsibility for any additional documentation necessary to ensure the grantee's title, such as releases from family members who should have signed the original transfer deed
- *covenant against encumbrances*, which means the grantor promises that any and all easements or liens have been properly disclosed and is liable for damages if others are discovered after the transfer

- *covenant of warranty forever*, or *warranty of title*, which means the grantor promises to bear the cost of defending the title against undiscovered or undisclosed flaws existing at the time of transfer – sometimes seen as synonymous with the covenant of quiet enjoyment

*As stated in the preceding Topic Area on Title Insurance, regardless of which type of deed is used to convey and/or warrant title, there may be a **defect in the title** that prevents the absolute legal conveyance of clear title.*

VIII-C. Escrow or Closing; Tax Aspects of Transferring Title to Real Property
(Expect 1-2 questions from this area)

Escrow is a generic legal term used to refer to both (1) *an account,* as in, "We put the rent deposit money in escrow." In this sense, escrow is interchangeable with *escrow account*, *impound account*, and, in some states, *trust account*, and (2) *the 'signed-contract to delivered-deed' period* of a real estate transaction, as in, "The property is in escrow."

> ***Real Estate Settlement Procedures Act (RESPA)*** *literature states that the terms "'settlement' and 'closing' can be and are used interchangeably."*

> *However, **since the PSI outline uses the term "escrow"** for this Topic Area, wherever its meaning could be interpreted as referring to the 2nd meaning above, **simply accept it as a synonymous term for the settlement/closing process**.*

*Also, despite local preferences and conventions that use one over the other, in most cases here, and perhaps on the PSI exam, **"settlement" will be used instead of "closing,"** if for no other reason than because it is the term printed prominently on every **"Settlement Statement (HUD-1)"** form nationwide; **this form is still in use**, though the **Closing Disclosure (CD) form** is replacing it in most residential transactions.*

The *purpose of settlement* is to **consummate the transaction** by **fulfilling the contract conditions, disbursing required funds, and transferring title**.

> *Some settlement conventions and processes vary from state to state. For example, in some states lawyers are an integral part of closings whereas they are rarely involved in any part of a routine transaction in others.*

> *Due to such differences in practice, details that are not uniform nationwide will not be tested on the general exam, but may appear on the state-specific exam if they are tested at all. Nevertheless, certain terms or processes may appear in distractors.*

So, take note of the following terms
- *settlement agent* is the term for to the party authorized to process the closing/settlement details, regardless of whether it would be a lawyer, a title company representative, an 'escrow agent,' or another official by any name
- *escrow/trust account* is the term you might see rather than escrow or trust account to refer to a **property sales transaction account** – this term **clarifies, for testing purposes, the interchangeable nature of these terms** and *allows all candidates to readily*

understand, within the context of question, that the question is about a sales transaction situation rather than an office trust account question.

The settlement agent acts in a fiduciary capacity regarding all transaction funds and details.

Further, the settlement agent oversees the checklist of details and contingencies created by the ***sales contract*** and ***loan-related specifics***. These may include such elements as

- securing the ***satisfaction and release of contingencies***
- verifying the documentation necessary for the ***satisfaction and release of liens***
- gathering and reviewing documents regarding ***encumbrances, restrictions, title and property insurance***, and other contract-specific requirements
- ***disbursing transaction funds*** according to ***priority of liens***, which generally get paid, first to last, in the following order
    - ***property taxes***
    - ***special assessments***
    - ***first mortgage***
    - ***other liens***, generally by date of recordation
    - ***other closing/settlement fees***
    - ***balance***, if any, ***to the seller***, or ***foreclosed owner in a forced sale***
- ***recordation*** of pertinent documents, e.g., releases for any extinguished lien(s) and/or encumbrance(s); new deed and lien(s)
- ***filing IRS form 1099-S, Proceeds from Real Estate Transaction***, with the IRS and getting a copy to the seller for reporting on the seller's tax returns

A settlement statement is the document that provides ***the transaction's final, detailed accounting summary***. The particular form of the settlement statement may ***vary from state to state as well as from transaction to transaction***.

However, a "default" for references to settlement statements will be either the ***Closing Disclosure (CD)*** or the uniform ***Settlement Statement (HUD-1)***, or just ***HUD-1***, since they are used nationwide for residential loans governed by the Real Estate Settlement Procedures Act (RESPA).

A list of ***critical documents*** that are commonly included in the closing process for the sale of a residential property secured by a loan would, at a minimum, be likely to include

- ***RESPA settlement and disclosure documents as required***
- ***deed*** for the real property included in the transaction
- ***bill(s) of sale*** for all ***personal (unattached) property*** included in the transaction
    *It is worth repeating here that **real property ownership is transferred by a deed**, while the **transfer of personal property ownership** is formally accomplished through a **bill of sale**. Both provide evidence that **title** has also been passed.*
- ***title insurance policy(ies)*** as required
- ***property insurance*** as required
- ***reduction certificate***, which is a loan document that shows the remaining principal balance, interest rate, and date of maturity; it is used by a seller who needs to know the exact payoff amount on the day of closing as well as to verify the terms and amount of an existing loan that a buyer may be assuming

- *satisfaction piece*, or *satisfaction of mortgage*, which is the certificate a mortgagee provides to a mortgagor that states the debt has been paid; typically it is recorded to confirm the title is free of the seller's mortgage lien's encumbrance
- *estoppel certificate*, or *offset statement*, or *certificate of no defense*, *which is a statement from a tenant or a mortgagee attesting to relevant conditions, such as the tenant's security deposit or a mortgage's balance, that is used to stop the party from claiming different facts later*
- *IRS form 1099-S* for reporting the proceeds of the sale

Many of the costs involved in a real estate transfer *are negotiable*, even when convention has one party or the other as typically responsible.

Closing costs as presented on the closing/settlement statement are commonly referred to as *credits* and *debits*, which means, respectively, that funds are *due and payable to a particular party* or that funds are *to be provided by a particular a party.*

Common costs and responsible parties include
- *buyer's closing costs*, where applicable
    - *refunds to seller* of prorated portion of remaining fuel oil and other prepaid utility and property expenses
    - *deed and new mortgage recording fees*
    - *appraisal fees for loan funding*
    - *home inspection fees*
    - *new loan or assumption fees*
- *seller's closing costs*, where applicable
    - *cost of clearing title*
    - *loan payoff*
    - *termite inspection*
    - *broker's commission*

While some questions in this area will focus on which party is responsible for certain charges, who pays how much will be addressed in the appropriate Topic Area of Outline Section X, Real Estate Calculations.

Most tax aspects of property transfers are locally controlled revenue generators, so cannot be tested in this Topic Area; such state or municipality specific questions may appear in the State-specific portion of the exam, or as a math question with all of the variables provided.

Internal Revenue Service (IRS) capital gains allowances generally top the list of test questions about the *tax aspects of property transfer*.

Broadly speaking, IRS capital gains on a property are computed by subtracting the actual sales price a seller gets from the amount the seller bought the property for earlier.

*In practice, it would typically take an accountant to compute the reportable capital gain—or loss—after subtracting the original purchase price, cost of improvements, and other deductible expenses, from the gross proceeds as reported on **IRS Form 1099-S, Proceeds from Real Estate Transaction**.*

Questions on capital gains for residential properties will be based on the ***Taxpayer Relief Act of 1997***, which says that on the sale of a ***primary residence*** that has been ***owner-occupied for two of the past five years***, the owner(s) are allowed to exempt capital gains of

- ***$250,000 for a single seller***, or
- ***$500,000 for a married couple filing jointly***

The Act also specifies that these ***exempt sales can be repeated***, and so creates incentives for certain kinds of real estate speculation; previously, capital gains in the same range had to be reinvested within a specified post-sale period to remain exempt.

The provisions of the 1997 Act are in stark contrast to ***the law it replaced***, which ***allowed homeowners over 55*** years of age a ***once-in-a-lifetime exclusion of $125,000 worth of capital gains*** on the sale of a primary residence.

> *The particulars of the outdated law are noted here in case they appear as distractors, as well as to clue you in when a client, acquaintance, or even an older family member makes reference to "that once-in-a-lifetime thing"—it happened to me not very long ago!*

As noted in Topic Area IV-A, General Concepts (of Financing), ***IRS tax issues*** regarding the costs, benefits, and tax implications of property financing include the following borrower-related items that are worth remembering during a property transfer

- ***interest payments*** on mortgage loans are deductible if the owner itemizes deductions, though for homeowners with low-balance loans and few other deductions, the standard deduction may be better than itemizing
- ***real estate taxes*** are deductible
- ***certain costs*** of financing and refinancing may be deductible, such as ***origination fees***, ***discount points***, and loan ***prepayment penalties***

Another common property-related tax matter is the ***1031 exchange***. Named for the Internal Revenue Code Section 1031, it refers to situations where an investor takes the ***proceeds from a property sale and defers paying capital gains taxes by reinvesting the funds in different, but like-kind properties***.

> *Not surprisingly, 1031 exchanges have a whole set of rules, such as a **time limit for qualifying reinvestment purchases** and numerous accounting details, that are too complex for entry-level licensure testing; some regulators would argue that even simple definition questions on this topic should only be used on broker exams.*

> *However, since 1031 exchanges are not uncommon in practice, you should be familiar with the basic concept. Besides, the term may appear as a distractor!*

> > ***Boot*** *is another term commonly associated with 1031 exchanges for **additional cash** required over the reinvestment amount from sold properties. However, it typically refers to any cash or other goods added to any transaction to make up for differences between a new property's value and funds available from a sold/exchanged property.*

Special reminder: to limit your liability as well as ensure greater accuracy, refer clients to an accountant or tax attorney for answers to tax-related questions.

VIII-D. Special Processes   (Expect 0-2 question from this area)

Foreclosure is an area of special note since it is the most common recourse for lenders, and refers to the legal proceeding initiated by certain property creditors to *force the sale of a property in default on a loan or in arrears for taxes in order to repay the debt.*

A foreclosure sale is an example of *involuntary alienation, or involuntary transfer, of property ownership.*

Foreclosure types and processes are too varied and state-specific to address here, though it is worth noting that the two-party mortgage and the three-party deed of trust have different basic sets of processes

- *generally, the processes are known, respectively, as (1) **judicial**, which means by a legal action in court that results in **a sale by court order**, or **writ of execution**, and (2) **nonjudicial**, which means things proceed according to contract terms alone*
- *at a settlement for a foreclosure sale, the **priority of liens**, or the order of repayment to creditors with the sale proceeds, is important; if the proceeds do not cover all property liens, the creditors may be entitled to seek a **deficiency judgment** against the foreclosed property owner*

Depending on the particular case as well as the state in which the foreclosure occurs, some form of the following types of *protections* and/or *remedies* for *the owner* may come into play.

*Since many of the following terms, concepts, and processes are not uniformly available or applied nationwide, **they are provided for informational purposes and may be used on exams as distractors**. Their specific applicability in your own state, however, may make them a part of your state-specific exam.*

Some common terms associated with *alternatives to foreclosure*, *homeowner protections*, and *other remedies* include

- *forbearance*, which refers to an alternative by which the creditor refrains from taking legal action against a borrower in default after being satisfied that the borrower is taking acceptable measures to satisfy the debt; commonly referred to as *workout*, forbearance may involve adjustments to the payment schedule or amounts due, as well as some other negotiated *mortgage modification*
- a *deed in lieu of foreclosure*, or *deed in lieu*, and also known as a *"friendly foreclosure,"* is, as the name suggests, a situation in which the owner gives a lender the deed rather than going through a foreclosure proceeding
- *redemption*, which refers to the right to pay off a debt, even after mortgage default, and reclaim the property; this remedy varies widely in its particulars
  - *redemption rights vary from state to state, but may include a before-foreclosure-sale right known as the **equitable right of redemption**, or even a statutory period after a sale, known as a **statutory right of redemption***
- *homestead laws*, in states where they exist, such as Florida, may provide a *homestead protection* that shields part or all of a residence against creditors. This protection is often referred to as a *homestead exemption*, because the protection may 'exempt' property from creditor attachment

- however, **'exemption'** more widely refers to any homestead <u>tax exemption</u> **program(s)** available from an owner's state or local taxation authorities that reduces the annual property tax for qualifying owners, **generally based on income, age, veteran status, or handicap**
- **tenant rights** regarding **leased occupancy of a foreclosed property** were introduced both federally and in many state laws in the wake of the subprime mortgage crisis. **From May 2009 through the end of 2014, properties with federally-related mortgages**, federal law required lenders to honor existing leases and/or provide at least **ninety (90) days' notice of intention to terminate**, depending on the specific circumstances
  - **The federal law was only effective through the end of 2014.** However, efforts have been advanced to reinstate this on the federal level, so keep abreast of developments to reinstate this protection. Tenant protections during foreclosure have requirements that should be reviewed by a tenant's legal counsel to ensure the tenant's particular situation is interpreted correctly, and subsequent rights and protections are upheld.

A **short sale** is another alternative to foreclosure on certain distressed properties that have a ready, qualified buyer; it involves the sale of the property with a lender-approved reduction, often about 20%, of the outstanding mortgage balance, and can also involve new-owner assumption of the reduced mortgage

- short sales typically involve a lawyer negotiating with the lender on the actual reduction amount; short sales can benefit the lender financially by avoiding the cost of full foreclosure and subsequent property maintenance, marketing, and sales commission expenses, as well as possible lender accounting benefits

With the well-publicized rise in home foreclosures stemming from both subprime loans and prime loans on properties that have lost significant value, you are likely to see the terms **"upside down"** or **"underwater"** for properties with **property values that have dropped below their mortgage balance**.

These terms, now much more mainstream than ever before, may appear in test questions that describe particular distressed property scenarios and then ask you to identify resolution options for either the lender or the borrower.

Real Estate Owned (REO) properties are a relatively new specialty area for real estate licensees, and typically refer to bank-owned properties that have come under their management when a lender's foreclosure action did not result in a sale and a mortgagor does not find a way to reclaim the property.

REOs are a source of business for property managers and others who specialize in **property preservation**, since financial lenders need to provide maintenance and security as well as property-specific rehabilitation to their REO properties in order to attract new owners.

The terms and processes given below, especially voluntary and involuntary transfers, are basic real estate material, some of which PSI may test and tally in other Topic Areas.

So **you would be well-advised to read what follows**. Even if there are no questions on the Salesperson exam regarding these processes, you should be familiar with the information below, *since some of the associated terms are likely to appear as distractors, and more importantly, in your upcoming professional life.*

The *transfer*, or *alienation*, or *conveyance* of title to property ownership from one party to another can be categorized as being either *voluntary* or *involuntary*.

*The terms **transfer** and **alienation** are interchangeable, so either one may appear in test questions; **alienation** is used almost exclusively when property transfers are **involuntary**.*

Voluntary transfer refers to the free-will transfer of property by its owner using methods such as
- *deeding* it after selling it or making it a gift
- *assigning* it to another
- *dedicating* it for public use
- *willing* it to an heir

Property *dedication* refers to the donation of private property for public use. For example, a developer may *dedicate* roads and some common-use areas in a subdivision as part of its plan, so the municipality will own and maintain them.

Also, if the public uses *nondedicated* private land as if it were public, the property may become subject to a municipal easement, much like a prescriptive easement for individual users, and legally turn into *dedicated property*.

Note: All over the country, there are privately owned roads, public places, and sections of sidewalks that the owners may mark somehow as "nondedicated property" and/or actually close off to the public one day a year to interrupt public use and thereby demonstrate such use has been allowed under a revocable license. By doing this, the owner helps avoid loss of control through a claim of dedication.

Involuntary transfer, or *involuntary alienation*, refers to any situation where *title transfers* in a manner that the owner may not have any control over or would generally prefer not to have happen. Examples of these would include
- *foreclosure* due to financial default, including tax sales
  - *distress sale is a term applied to most forced or below-market property sales; distress sales have become a strong niche market in the real estate industry*
- *condemnation* through the process of *eminent domain*
  - *inverse condemnation, which is when the owner forces a governmental agency to either step-up the payment on a condemned property or actually condemn it due to a court-determined decline in use or value based on some governmental action, like building a military airport right next to the owner's residence*
- *escheat* due to an owner's dying intestate with no heirs
- *adverse possession* as a result of a court's approval that a claimant deserves to acquire title to a property due to legally adequate and compelling *open, notorious, and hostile* use of a particular property for a statutory period
- *partition* by a court-ordered sale of a property with multiple owners, one or more of which cannot get the other(s) to buy their interest, and so petition the court to force a sale in order to receive their share of the proceeds
- *reversion* due to a breach in the terms of the deed or contract

Finally, the **transfer of property by inheritance** involves some "special process" terms that are worth noting here. Some of these are

- **testate** refers to **having a will**; a **testator** is someone who has made a will
- **intestate** refers to a situation where **a person dies without a valid will**
- **probate** is the public, legal process of executing the terms outlined in a will, or determining how to settle the estate if there is no will
  - **personal representative** is, in more and more states, the person designated to see that the terms of a will are carried out; or the following names may apply
    - an **executor** is/was the term for a personal representative **appointed by the testator in the will** to execute the terms of the will; the term **executrix** refers to a female representative, *though* **executor** *is increasingly used in a gender-neutral way to identify this position*
    - an **administrator** is/was the term for a personal representative **appointed by probate when someone died intestate, or when there is a will and the court sees a reason to appoint an administrator**; the term **administratrix** refers to a female representative, *though* **administrator** *is increasingly used in a gender-neutral way to identify this position*
  - **intestate succession** refers to the distribution of an estate that is not governed by a will, and follows state **laws of descent and distribution** (or **devise and descent**) for **intestacy**
    - **escheat**, as noted above, is the process of property reverting to the state in the event someone dies intestate and with no heirs
- **types of wills** include
  - **formal**, *or witnessed, which are typically prepared with the help of an attorney*
  - **holographic**, *or handwritten and unwitnessed*
  - **oral**, *or* **nuncupative**, *which is a will spoken by the person who is near death and written down by a witness*
- **real** *property disposed of in a will* is known as a **devise**; the recipient is a **devisee**
- **personal** *property disposed of in a will* is known as a **legacy** or **bequest**; the recipient is a **legatee**
- **real property transfers** to a devisee or a buyer in order to pay estate obligations may be **conveyed by** an **executor's deed** or an **administrator's deed**, depending on whether or not there is a will
  - *State-specific terms for conveyance instruments that transfer title of certain properties, especially family-retained property, of a deceased owner vary. Documents issued by probate courts generally function legally as quitclaim deeds granted either directly by or on behalf of the deceased. Check with a real estate attorney for other available transfer instruments and applicable terms.*

This ends the presentation of key terms and concepts likely to be either tested or used as distractors in this Content Outline Section.

IX-A. Trust/Escrow Accounts (General) *[Regulatory Details in State Portion]*
(Expect 1-2 questions from this area)

This area presents, in a general way, the ***common law basics of trust accounts*** and their use in ***ensuring that licensees faithfully observe their fiduciary duty of accounting for transaction funds.*** *As noted in the heading, regulatory details will be found in the state portion of the exam.*

However, in general, ***the purpose of trust, or escrow, accounts*** is to provide an account that is ***separate from operational or personal accounts*** in which ***to maintain and account for transaction-related funds.***

Typically the are required to be opened in a bank doing business in the licensee's state, and are the responsibility of the firm's primary broker to establish and oversee. Generally, even if the primary broker is allowed to delegate account management, the ultimate responsibility—and liability—for proper handling of monies remains at the top.

Questions in this area will be necessarily broad, and probably develop scenarios demonstrating expected standards of accounting.

Though licensees are often expected to submit all transaction-related funds to their broker and the funds are expected to be deposited within a statutory period, such as "three banking days" or "forty-eight-hours, excluding weekends and holidays," any questions about such details will be written using phrases like "within the required period" rather than a specific number of days

Though mentioned in the last Topic Area in outlining fiduciary duties, it is worth repeating that as a fiduciary, any licensee who accepts transaction-related funds has an obligation of ***accounting***, which means the licensee is obligated to avoid either of the following situations with those funds

- ***commingling***, which means mingling, or combining, transaction funds with other funds that are required to be maintained separately; this could result from putting the funds in the wrong account, either business or personal
- ***conversion***, which refers to ***converting funds to another use than the one intended by the principal***, or ***misappropriating them***, as in using earnest money to pay office expenses ***or for any personal use***; conversion is generally preceded by commingling

*Additional particulars regarding the **handling of monies**, such as **to whom it is given**, **into which account it gets deposited**, the **time period within which it must be deposited**, and **method(s) of disbursal, especially when there is a dispute**, are all state-specific and may be tested on the state portion of the exam.*

Remember that even though licensees have specific fiduciary duties to a client, they owe the obligations of ***honesty and fair dealing*** to all parties, including customers, and this extends to handling any customer funds entrusted to the licensee.

Further, review your own state statutes governing accounts and recordkeeping to determine the regulatory requirements for holding and maintaining transaction funds as well as tenant deposits; for example, some states that have Landlord/Tenant Acts often require deposits be held in an account that bears nominal interest for the tenant.

And each state has its own requirements for which records to maintain, acceptable methods to store them, such as electronic or original hard copy, and how long they must be retained in the event the regulatory agency wants to examine them.

IX-B. Federal Fair Housing Laws

(Expect 3-4 questions from this area)

In a nutshell, the **Civil Rights Act** and the federal **Fair Housing Act** are terms that encompass and refer to all Fair Housing legislation, beginning with the **Civil Rights Act of 1866** through the federal **Fair Housing Act of 1968**, also known as **Title VIII of the Civil Rights Act of 1968**, and the federal **Fair Housing Amendments Act of 1988**. The **Americans with Disabilities Act (ADA)** is separate, though related, and deals with access to public buildings.

> **Note: You should NOT be tested on what specifically became protected at which time along the way.** *Despite any appearance to the contrary by the use of slightly different terms, test vendors have historically been aware that* **the real estate license exam is <u>not</u> the place for a mini-test on "The History and Evolution of the Fair Housing Law."**

> *Ultimately, a real estate licensee's obligation regarding Fair Housing is simple:* **do not discriminate**. *And just to be sure you know how to spot it when you see it, you should know the following basic protections, provisions, and violations.*

The **Civil Rights Act of 1866** asserted **one basic protection**: there was to be **no race-based discrimination in the housing market**. The U. S. Supreme Court decision of **Jones v. Mayer (1968)** reaffirmed this position as the law of the land.

The accumulated provisions of the federal **Fair Housing Amendments Act of 1988** include prohibiting discrimination in the sale, rental, or advertising of residential property for **protected classes** based on the following personal characteristics
  - *race or color*
  - *national origin*
  - *religious preference*
  - *sex*
  - *handicapping conditions*, which means having a physical or mental disability, including infection with the HIV virus or recovery status for drug and alcohol dependence, that substantially limits one or more major life activity
  - *familial status*, which means *one or more individuals under 18 years of age being domiciled* with a parent or custodian, or the legal designee of the parents, and also *applies to any person who is pregnant* or in the process of securing legal custody of any individual under 18 years old
    - *older persons exemption* to familial status protection for multi-unit properties *may apply* to housing that is
      - intended for and *solely occupied by* persons *62 years of age or older*
      - intended for older persons and *80 percent or more of the units* are occupied by *at least one occupant 55 years of age or older*

Practices that would be *violations* of Fair Housing laws include
- *steering*, which means showing prospective buyers of a particular protected class properties only in areas that have a high representation of the same class
- *blockbusting*, which means 'spreading the word' that property values may decline due to an increased presence in the area of a particular protected class, so owners should consider selling before the 'price drop'
  - *this may also be called **panic-peddling**, or **panic selling**, under which there may be no discrimination involved in a licensee's marketing based on a fear of falling prices; examples include real or trumped-up anticipation of change, such as a zoning change allowing a low-income housing project in an affluent neighborhood*
- *redlining*, which applies to a *lender's* designation of a particular area as a 'loan-free zone' due to the presence in that area of a protected class

Federal Fair Housing laws are *administered and enforced by the Department of Housing and Urban Development (HUD),* which also provides an *Equal Housing Opportunity poster* for real estate offices. *(Note: HUD complaints are investigated by the Office of Fair Housing and Equal Opportunity (FHEO).)*

*This **HUD poster** is expected to be **displayed prominently** in the office as a statement that the office supports non-discriminatory practices in housing sales and rentals. **Its absence** can be used against the office broker and/or other licensees being investigated for discrimination by HUD as **evidence of discriminatory practices**.*

The HUD symbol and an anti-discrimination notice are often included in company listing forms, marketing materials, and advertising as a further demonstration that the company and its licensees adhere to Fair Housing guidelines.

Be sure that in preparing all materials and advertising that no language is used that singles out any protected class, regardless of whether it is offering discounts or discouragement – and watch on the test for questions that ask you to identify an example of acceptable, discrimination-free advertising!

Some property transactions are exempt from federal Fair Housing laws. These include
- *sale or rental of a single-family dwelling by owner* without a real estate licensee's involvement
- *rental of rooms or units in one- to four-family dwellings if one is owner-occupied*
- *preferences shown by a religious organization for its own members* in the sale, rental, or occupancy of real estate, as long as the organization does not restrict membership based on any of the protected classes
- *preferences shown by a private club for its own members* in a rental or occupancy of residential real estate, as long as the club is not open to the public and the lodging is not operated commercially

The sale or rental of a single-family dwelling unit is *NOT exempt from Fair Housing laws whenever there is a real estate licensee involved*, and
- under the Civil Rights Act, even properties exempt from Fair Housing laws are *protected against discrimination whenever it is based on race*

Important Fair Housing note for property rentals: In residential property rentals covered by Fair Housing requirements, a *landlord must allow a handicapped tenant to make __reasonable modifications__ to a unit __at the tenant's own expense__*, typically *with the obligation to return the unit to its previous condition when moving out.*

Special clarification: This requirement is based on Fair Housing laws, NOT the Americans With Disabilities Act (ADA) requirements, which apply to public accessibility.

The *Americans with Disabilities Act (ADA)* includes provisions for *handicapped access and accommodations in public buildings*. This includes ramps, wheelchair-accessible rest room facilities, and elevators. It also has a host of details that are more appropriately the responsibility of developers, builders, and architects rather than real estate licensees. However, a few key definitions, concepts, and requirements include

- *disability* means a *physical or mental impairment that substantially limits one or more major life activities*
- *places of public accommodation include real estate offices*
- *employers with 15 or more employees* must comply with ADA requirements for both nondiscriminatory employment practices and employee workplace accommodations

IX-C. Advertising and Technology   (Expect 1-3 questions from this area)

As noted in the previous Topic Area, a licensee needs to observe Fair Housing guidelines when advertising properties for sale or rent, so Fair Housing questions on advertising may be tallied in this area. And there are other federal requirements for certain types of advertising, especially loan terms (see below) as well as additional requirements in the state-specific portion of most state outlines, commonly that a licensee must include the agency's name in ads.

But the most likely area where a licensee could go afoul of acceptable guidelines is in simple property descriptions. Advertisements typically engage in some form of highly subjective "property enhancement," sometimes referred to as *puffing* or *puffery*, by describing run-down properties as "handyman specials," small homes as having a "modest floor plan," or a site as offering "the best view of the mountain" compared to others with arguably similar views.

*So, questions in this area may also focus on examples or definitions of **puffing** or **puffery**. They may also ask you to determine whether a misleading description is based on poor information, and possibly just **negligent misrepresentation**, or **willful misrepresentation**.*

*For example, advertising a property as having a 1,520 square foot floor plan is a verifiable fact. If a licensee's advertisement presents this as "nearly 2,000 square feet!" the licensee may be guilty of **misrepresentation** rather than just engaging in puffery.*

*However, if a buyer then relies on that statement as a fact and the licensee **deliberately avoids correcting the "fact"** before the buyer is damaged by relying on that information, it is quite likely that a judge would rule the licensee had gone beyond **deliberate misrepresentation** and had ultimately committed **fraud**.*

Under the provisions of the *Federal Trade Commission Act*, there are specific *truth-in-advertising* rules and guidelines. These include requiring advertisers to ensure that

- *advertising must be truthful and non-deceptive,* which means that the ad includes no statement, and omits no information, that is either likely to mislead or material to misleading consumers
- *advertisers must have evidence to back up their claims*, and
- *advertisements cannot be unfair*, which means it causes or is likely to cause unavoidable consumer injury

The federal *Truth in Lending Act (TILA)*, a part of the *Consumer Credit Protection Act*, has a detailed set of loan *disclosure* and *advertising* requirements for lenders who originate residential loans. *Regulation Z* is the regulation that implements the Act and explains how lenders are to comply with those parts of TILA that bear on consumer credit.

> *Style Note: Testing convention combines these terms, making them the **Truth-in-Lending Act (Regulation Z)** for most test questions, especially those regarding Regulation Z. This ensures they are properly linked on the test as they are in practice, while avoiding both the possibility and the appearance of testing on which one does what, which are distinctions better left to lenders and lawyers.*

> *For clarity in presenting a general overview here, though, they will separated briefly; the test questions will typically bring them back together.*

TILA is intended to enable the customer to examine loan offers to determine
- the *cost of a cash-versus-credit transaction*
- the *difference in the cost of credit among different lenders*

Regulation Z is intended to spell out how to ensure that customers get meaningful, accurate, and complete information to make informed credit comparisons and decisions.

> *It is important for licensees to understand key elements of TILA and Regulation Z as they relate to mortgage loans in order to explain them to customers and clients.*

> *However, since they govern the professional activities of <u>lenders</u>, their intricacies **are not appropriate** for real estate examinations. (For example, they apply to certain other consumer credit transactions, but for our immediate purpose here, so what?)*

> *Key elements of TILA* are that it
> - is a *federal* law, though states may have their own adaptations
> - *seeks to ensure the informed use of consumer credit* by borrowers
> - requires lenders to provide *meaningful disclosures of credit terms and costs*
> - *applies to loans secured by a personal residence* (among others)

> *Key elements of Regulation Z* include that it
> - *provides the specific requirements of TILA*

- requires *disclosure standards for advertisements* when the ad includes details for certain credit terms, known as *trigger terms*. These include
  - *amount or percentage of down payment*
  - *amount of any payment*
  - *number of payments*
  - *period of repayment*
  - *dollar amount of finance charges, or that there is no charge for credit*

> An advertisement containing details for any of the above trigger terms, such as "only $500 down!" must *disclose* <u>*all*</u> of the following information
> - *down payment information*
> - *the cash price or loan amount*
> - *terms of repayment (number, amount, and schedule)*
> - *the annual percentage rate (APR) and possibility of any increases*
> - <u>*some*</u> sales also require the *total of all payments*

- requires lenders to make certain *disclosures on loans* within three business days after their receipt of a written application and again at the time of loan closing, if the loans are subject to the *Real Estate Settlement Procedures Act (RESPA)* – (see IV-F, Financing/Credit Laws for more on RESPA). There are over 18 required disclosures, which include *the amount financed, the finance charge, the annual percentage rate (APR),* and *the total of all payments*

- allows a borrower a *limited three-day right to rescind* a loan contract, or revoke it without penalty, after signing *for certain home improvement loans*, but *NOT* for a primary residential mortgage *(though some refinancing arrangements may invoke the rescission right)*

Remember the earlier note: real estate licensees are NOT lenders, who are the ones who need to know the fine-line, ever-changing details, such as the other 14+ RESPA disclosures. So do not panic over memorizing all 18+ disclosures -- review them if they are in your main textbook, then move on.

A final note on advertising: the laws above and any others require that *disclaimers and disclosures must be clear and conspicuous*, regardless of the medium, including the Internet.

Although *technology* is clearly driving and changing the way many real-estate-related tasks get done, the prelicensing exam is not the place to test a candidate's knowledge, skills, or abilities with software, Web platforms, or productivity gizmos.

Yet as both clients and companies become more tech-dependent in the performance of basic real estate functions, the exam has to remain open to including future basics once they uniformly affect entry-level licensees nationwide, especially with Web-based applications. This already includes such functions as marketing, researching property information, correspondence and contracts, and electronic filing of deeds and other land records.

Right now, *technology is most visibly applicable* to daily entry-level activities in the federal law that asserts legal status for properly sent and received *electronic documents*.

As noted earlier, a relatively recent federal Act has made certain electronic transmissions legally valid substitutes for hand-written signatures and hard-copy transaction documents. ***The Electronic Signatures in Global and National Commerce Act (ESIGN)*** (2000) defines and covers the legal force of electronic signatures in ***interstate and international commerce***.

> ***ESIGN states that*** in interstate and foreign commerce, signatures, contracts, and other ***transaction documents "may not be denied legal effect, validity, or enforceability solely because [they are] in an electronic form."*** It also provides for electronic storage and retention of these records.

> ***Increasingly, states are conforming with ESIGN standards by noting that the required records may be retained in any format, electronic or otherwise, capable of producing an accurate copy in paper format of the original document.***

> ***According to ESIGN, "electronic record"*** means a ***contract or other record created, generated, sent, communicated, received or stored by electronic means.***

> > Some states have specifically identified these records to include ***faxes***, ***email***, ***telexes***, and ***instant/Internet messages (IMs).*** Even though these are not specifically named in the federal law, they are each reasonably understood to be a type of "electronic record," so may appear in a question about the legality of relying on particular documents.

The ***Telephone Consumer Protection Act of 1991 (TCPA)*** and subsequent laws regulate telemarketing activities. Provisions include, among other measures, ***restricting the hours for calling (between 8 a.m. and 9 p.m. local time), maintaining a free "do-not-call list"*** for those who ask to be on it (***it takes 31 days after registering*** before complaints can be brought), and ***prohibiting recorded messages***, ***fax solicitations***, and ***automated dialing***, or ***"robocalls."***

- *The **Do Not Call Registry** is **managed by the Federal Trade Commission (FTC)** and **enforced by the Federal Communications Commission (FCC) and state-level agencies;** for more information and how to ensure your own real estate telemarketing conforms with the law (violations begin at $500-1,500/illegal call), see **www.donotcall.gov***

Further, there are numerous states that have enacted regulations governing ***advertising and marketing via Web postings*** for real estate listings and services, typically that the firm identify itself on every page as well as update information at specific intervals.

> ***One federal law is of special note here:***
> - <u>***C***</u>***ontrolling the*** <u>***A***</u>***ssault of*** <u>***N***</u>***on-***<u>***S***</u>***olicited*** <u>***P***</u>***ornography*** <u>***A***</u>***nd*** <u>***M***</u>***arketing Act of 2003,*** better known as the ***CAN-SPAM Act,*** is a federal regulation intended to ***curb spam by having a set of compliance requirements for commercial emails***. There are ***three broad compliance requirements***, each of which has more specific guidelines than those provided below, but basically commercial emails must "pass muster" regarding
>   - an ***unsubscribe option*** that must be ***honored within 10 business days***
>   - ***content compliance***, e.g., accurate "from" line, subject line relevant to content, and a legitimate physical address of the key party

- *sending compliance*, e.g., it must have at least one sentence of content, an unsubscribe option below the message, no false header, and cannot be sent to a harvested email address

*And, with the emergence of the many, many business and personal uses for **social media** and **ever-evolving platforms and apps** on the Internet, there are additional concerns regarding both **firm and individual liability for licensee texts, blogs, social media postings, videos, and other Internet exchanges**. Expect to see these addressed and routinely revised in Policy Manuals of real estate firms, and hear of new regulations and court cases for years!*

IX-D. Agent Supervision and Broker-Associate Relationship
(Expect 1-3 questions from this area)

This Topic Area is most likely to contain scenario and/or application questions about the liability a broker has for the actions of affiliated licensees. As noted previously, common *types of legal liabilities* include

- *vicarious*, which refers to a *supervisor* or *principal's responsibility* for the acts of a *subordinate* or *agent*, respectively; this is most commonly seen in the liability almost any employer has for the professional misdeeds of employees regardless of whether or not they were known to or authorized by the employer
  - *some states, but far from all, **have specifically abolished vicarious liability** in real estate transactions, especially broker liability for actions of their agents, noting that there is **"no imputation of knowledge" on the part of those parties not directly involved with the transaction***
- *joint*, which means *shared liability between two or more parties*
- *several*, which means a *liability of one party that can be legally pursued separately* from other liable parties

Most details about a broker's responsibility to supervise affiliated licensees, including providing them with office policies and training opportunities, are either state-specific or company-generated, so there is not much material available for general testing.

However, it is common for licensees to enter into an *independent contractor arrangement* with a *principal broker*, or *broker-in-charge*, or *designated broker*, or *broker-of-record*, or some other jurisdiction-specific term for the "boss" authorized to "employ" other licensees.

As independent contractors, licensees are responsible for sending in quarterly estimated taxes, paying self-employment taxes, and providing their own health insurance.

Federal requirements governing the relationship between a firm and its licensees are primarily seen in the IRS distinction of *employee* versus *self-employed*, or *independent contractor*, status for tax purposes. According to the government, a licensed real estate agent may be treated as self-employed if

- *substantially all pay* for services as a real estate agent *is directly related to sales or other output rather than to hours worked*

- the services are performed under a written contract that provides *the real estate agent will not be treated as an employee for federal tax purposes*

There are more extensive guidelines that clarify the distinction between an employee and an independent contractor. However, they generally point out that when acting as an independent contractor, a licensee does not receive health, vacation, sick-day, or other benefits from the agency.

Further, the licensee is allowed to work according to the licensee's own schedule and pay all self-employment, federal, and other taxes rather than having them withheld and processed by the agency.

Contractual agreements between a broker and a licensee are quite likely to require state-specific elements, such as making sure that a copy of the company's policy manual or other critical documents are included as part of the agreement. So, general questions on contract agreements are most likely to focus on the IRS distinctions given above.

*It is important to note that in some states, **brokers who establish independent contractor rather than employee relationships with affiliated licensees do NOT distance themselves against legal liability** for claims that may arise regarding licensee misdeeds.*

This distinction MAY be addressed as part of another question, such as the following:

Question: *Which of the following statements about the difference between a licensee who is an independent contractor rather than an employee is CORRECT?*

WRONG
Answer: *A broker is not legally liable for the professional actions of a licensee who is an independent contractor but is for licensees who are employees.*

This option would be wrong because it is not a uniformly correct statement nationwide.

*Neither is a requirement for a brokerage to carry **errors and omissions (E&O) insurance**, or require affiliated licensees to do so, though in some states it is a legislated requirement as a means of recovery if an important—and costly—transaction detail is overlooked.*

IX-E. Commissions and Fees (Expect 1-2 questions from this area)

Commission and fees are common components of ***compensation agreements***, which are increasingly reflecting a host of creative compensation arrangements nationwide, even though the traditional commission percentage arrangement is still quite common.

Compensation agreements detail elements like a ***commission percentage*** rate, who is entitled to collect, ***commission-splitting*** arrangements for ***cooperating brokers***, as well as other compensation arrangements, such as a ***flat-fee for services*** rather than a commission, or ***reimbursements*** for certain marketing expenses.

However, *compensation arrangements in a buyer agency agreement* can be complicated by whether or not the buyer pays the agent directly for specific assistance in locating and securing a property or allows the agent to collect a listed property's commission split.

Plus there has been a recent rise in *companies offering to help market property* under some form of *flat-fee for limited services*, often just signs, property information flyers, and a posting in a multiple listing service (MLS), rather than charging a conventional commission for conventional full-service marketing. Some such companies set charges based on a list of *fees-for-services* plus *reimbursements* for specified costs.

An *important consideration* in setting commissions and compensation arrangements has to do with *maintaining open market competition* rather than *agreeing with competitors to standardize rates and fees*, so as noted elsewhere, they are *established by negotiation* between the *principal and the agent*.

> *Standardized compensation arrangements invite scrutiny—and potential penalties—as violations of antitrust laws; this will receive elaboration in an upcoming Topic Area.*

The following compensation arrangements also invite scrutiny for their basic ethical nature and legality under antitrust laws, especially when they are undisclosed

- *referral fees*, which are fees earned by referring business to someone
- *kickbacks*, which means the return of a portion of a payment received by a vendor to another individual involved in the vendor's getting some business, especially when it is part of a secret agreement.

The best way to handle these situations is to avoid them. The next-best way to handle *any compensation payments to or from anyone*, be it a commission, referral fee, gift, bonus, *"finder's fee"* to unlicensed parties, or anything else of value, is to *get the written, informed consent of all parties* to the transaction, even if it is not a specific requirement in your state.

> *This practice may be a specific requirement in your state, but if not, is a good safeguard against basic misunderstandings and financial disputes anywhere.*

Compensation disputes often arise in cases where a licensee introduces a party to a property and then that party either buys through another licensee or finds a way to deal directly with the owner.

These disputes are often legally resolved based on the application of the concept of *procuring cause*, which refers to determining if a licensee's efforts were instrumental in leading to the sale of real estate and is therefore generally entitled to a commission.

The traditional test for procuring cause, and arguable entitlement for an earned commission, is finding a buyer who is *ready, willing, and able to meet the seller's terms*.

> *In some states this is determined by who introduced the buyer to a property, regardless of who actually writes the offers and counteroffers for the buyer.*

Also, in many states, finding a ready, willing, and able buyer who meets the seller's terms is all that is required for a licensee to be entitled to a commission.

*In those states, commonly referred to as **"procuring cause states,"** if the seller backs out of a contract, or refuses to accept an offer that meets the listing specifications, the licensee may be able to successfully sue for compensation.*

Further, many jurisdictions allow various forms of protection for licensees in the event a principal acts unethically by telling an interested buyer to wait until after the agency agreement period expires and then return as a "free" party to pursue the transaction without having to incur a sales commission.

*Commonly known as **broker protection clauses**, they may be written into agency employment contracts using language that reinforces the agent's right to collect a commission for particular sales that occur even after contract termination.*

They are generally market-area specific, and may include a definite post-contract time period during which a sale still entitles the original agent to compensation. Such protection clauses may also involve a "protected persons" list of those who were introduced to the property by the agent, so could entitle the agent to compensation if one of them purchases the property.

*Over twenty states also have **broker lien laws** that generally cover a commercial agent's right to put a lien on a property when the owner fails to pay rental commissions. **In some states, though, the applicability of the law extends to all types of property transactions, so check your own state's lien laws.***

IX-F. General Ethics   (Expect 1-3 questions from this area)

This Topic Area is most likely to contain scenario and/or application questions that refer to ethical choices based on material covered in other Topic Areas, most notably Section V, General Principles of Agency, as well as the other Topic Areas in this Section.

For example, the question posed in the Agency area regarding a couple asking for advice about how to take title could be written to fit in this Topic Area by having the licensee provide a definitive answer without recommending they confirm it with an attorney.

*The licensee's definitive response **exceeds the licensee's authority**, and represents both **unethical behavior** and the **illegal practice of law**. Further, the licensee may be subject to legal action later on if the buyers relied on the information and were damaged by it.*

Additional topic treatments that raise ethical issues could include situations illustrating self-dealing, conflicts of interest, net listings, nondisclosure of agency relationships, misrepresentation of material facts, antitrust arrangements, and kickbacks, among others.

Agency duties include recognizing circumstances under which licensees should **refer parties to other professionals** for advice that exceeds the **limits of their professional competence or expertise** and **license authority**.

There are numerous examples in this area, such as referring parties to

- *real estate lawyers* for legal opinions on types of deeds or property restrictions
- *accountants or tax attorneys* for detailed financial and tax advice
- *surveyors* for property boundary and encroachment questions
- *home inspectors* for detailed property reports
- *appraisers* for property valuation
- *other professionals* as appropriate

For example, in most states, real estate sales contracts and many other transaction documents must be prepared by attorneys, and then simply used by licensees. In such states, preparing these documents may constitute grounds for *practicing law without a license*.

At least one state, Arizona, specifically authorizes licensees to draft sales contracts from scratch, so test questions on this are likely to specify that it might be beyond a licensee's authority or expertise to draft an especially complicated document.

Remember, failure to recommend the appropriate professional could mislead and harm a party, who in turn could take legal action against the licensee.

In addition, the exam may ask identification and recognition questions on such matters as *how to take title,* or *the use of preprinted forms,* or *the need to get the principals to initial any changes to contracts.*

Exam, and professional practice, note: the exam may ask identification and recognition questions on the above matters, such as

Question: *M and K took title in such a way that (plug in some description of ownership here). Which of the following terms identifies this type of ownership?*

Answer: *The answer would simply be a matter of fact, not opinion, and be based on a term and its definition that would be supported by textbooks and legal dictionaries alike.*

However, as a professional, it is important to protect yourself against giving advice that might present legal trouble, such as explaining different ways to hold title in a way that also sounds like a <u>recommendation</u> of how to take title.

Or sounding like the last word on a property's physical condition, or real estate tax matters, or anything else that, in short, exceeds the limits of your professional authority or expertise.

So, on the test, watch out for application-type questions, such as

Question: *M and K are interested in taking title in such a way that (plug in some description of ownership here) and ask the licensee who is working as their agent which form of ownership they should use. Which of the following statements indicates the licensee's BEST response?*

Answer: **For this question, the answer will probably identify the form that they have described, <u>but should include</u> a recommendation to seek an attorney's advice.**

If it does not, it leaves you, as a test-taker, with the incorrect impression that giving legal advice is just part of the real estate licensee's job. Such a question would itself be questionable, and quite remiss in its duties to both test and instruct.

In practice, be careful even if you have other professional credentials -- there's a difference between "speaking as an agent" and "speaking as an attorney."

Some *federal marketing controls* that serve as guidelines for ethical and legal behavior in the course of real estate transactions include such regulations as the following, most of which are of greater importance to experienced licensees and brokers than to entry-level licensees. These controls and regulations include

- *Truth in Lending Act (TILA), Regulation Z*, which has to do with lending practices and advertising *(discussed above)*
- *Equal Employment Opportunity Commission (EEOC)*, which is responsible for enforcing federal laws that make it illegal to discriminate against a job applicant or an employee because of the person's race, color, religion, sex (including pregnancy), national origin, age (40 or older), disability or genetic information
  - *it is also illegal to discriminate against a person because the person complained about discrimination, filed a charge of discrimination, or participated in an employment discrimination investigation or lawsuit*
  - *most employers with at least 15 employees are subject to EEOC requirements, for age discrimination cases it is 20 or more employees*
- *Uniform Commercial Code (UCC)*, which is a "uniform act," or proposed set of laws, that most states have adopted to govern commercial transactions of moveable, personal property, *including secured transactions*, such as ones in which a fixture, like a new heat pump, is purchased under a financing agreement and may be considered personal, 'detachable' property under a *security agreement* and/or *financing statement* until it is paid off
  - the *Bulk Sales Act* is Article VI of the Code, and covers *the transfer of inventory in order to avoid fraudulent conveyances designed to defraud creditors;*
    - *the UCC is most applicable for licensees that go into commercial real estate and need to know more about their clients' business environment; any test questions on the Code or its Bulk Sales Act are most likely to be marked for broker-exams only*
- *Interstate Land Sales Full Disclosure Act*, which *requires land developers to register certain large subdivisions with HUD and provide each purchaser with a disclosure document called a Property Report* before the signing of the contract or agreement; some states have their own adaptation of the federal Act
- the *Securities and Exchange Commission (SEC)* establishes *federal securities regulations*, some of which *apply to real estate investments that can be categorized as a security*, such as some limited partnerships in real estate; *selling such securities requires a securities license*
  - state legislation governing securities transactions are known as *"Blue Sky Laws"*

IX-G. Antitrust Laws   (Expect 1-2 questions from this area)

Compensation arrangements and marketing practices are governed by federal and state *antitrust laws*. Federal antitrust law is grounded in the Sherman Antitrust Act (1890) and the Clayton Antitrust Act (1914), commonly referred to as the *Sherman Antitrust Act*, or just *antitrust law*.

The primary purpose of antitrust law is to outlaw illegal monopolies, or monopolies that could be shown to be using their power to squelch competition; its primary lasting effect has been to stimulate open competition through regulating business practices that attempt to monopolize the market. The key terms that arise in antitrust considerations include

- ***monopoly***, which means that one firm or person is the only player in a particular business
- ***price-fixing***, which means that selected competitors agreeing to standardize prices as a way to reduce or remove additional competition by restricting the prices available for the consumer
- ***market allocation***, which occurs when competitors agree to parcel up market areas and only do business in their designated area, leaving it free from competition in exchange for not encroaching on the competitor's 'protected' zone
- ***boycotting***, which occurs when a group of competitors band together to refuse to either do business with or recommend the services of a particular company
- ***tie-in agreement***, or ***tying arrangement***, which refers to the practice of requiring a party to use a particular service or vendor, such as a lender requiring a borrower to hire a particular home inspector or closing attorney

Antitrust laws regarding price-fixing make it ***illegal for competing real estate companies to standardize commission rates*** or brokerage compensation arrangements. Rather, as noted above, ***they are established by negotiation between the principal and the agent***.

It is worth noting here that there are significant court precedents nationally that have upheld verdicts against licensees for antitrust violations in their business conduct.

Some cases are based in situations where "the word was out" about the "local" commission rate, i.e., price-fixing, but no formal "agreement" among the competing agencies which uniformly adopted the same rate was found.

Penalties have included felony convictions and significant damage awards.

The following compensation arrangements also invite scrutiny for their basic ethical nature and legality under antitrust laws, especially when they are undisclosed

- *referral fees*, which are fees earned by referring business to someone, and may be seen as a violation of antitrust laws if they are related to a tie-in agreement
- *kickbacks*, which means the return of a portion of a payment received by a vendor to another individual involved in the vendor's getting some business, especially when it is part of a secret agreement. Like a referral fee, it may be a violation of antitrust laws if it is part of a tie-in agreement.

This ends the presentation of key terms and concepts likely to be either tested or used as distractors in this Content Outline Section.

General comments about this Section, and about real estate Math

There are five Topic Areas specifically labeled in the PSI Content Outline Real Estate Calculations Section; there are six test questions from the entire Section.

Hmmm . . . simple math tells us that asking six questions from five Topic Areas means that only about eight percent (7.5% to be precise) of your total test score rides on doing math.

Further, if every Topic Area gets one question, only one Topic Area is likely to get even two questions on the test.

So, relax, and do NOT let the list of math topics make you think there is too much math to master – though you <u>should</u> know everything, you <u>do not need to</u> in order to pass!

Most of the six math questions on the test will not be particularly complicated. Those that are simply require you to take a deep breath and think a little harder.

Also, in most cases the questions will include all the numbers, conditions, and other information necessary to perform the math, as well as all conditions of who pays for what and whether prorations are based on 30-day versus 31-day months and 360-day versus 365-day years.

As for individual questions, the chances are good that you will be able to at least rule out a few of the answer choices and then be able to make a better-odds guess at whatever's left.

Special Note: PSI's math questions typically use "none of the above" as the fourth option.

*This means **you MUST be confident** in the answer you arrive at through your computations, since **the correct answer MAY NOT be among those given** and your answer may be based on a commonly made math error.*

So be careful and double-check your work for the greatest confidence in your conclusions.

For those of you with math anxiety, one strategy for tackling them is to mark them on the testing device with the colored "Mark" key as soon as they appear, then move on immediately to the next non-math question.

After answering all of the <u>non-math</u> questions, you can then return to <u>JUST</u> the "marked" questions and work them as a group, doing the ones that look easiest first.

The sub-topics presented in this outline section are bulleted below with a brief, "textbook-reminder" definition; ***additional related sub-topics*** are also included where they may be relevant, and testable.

If you need a more detailed explanation to perform a particular type of math computation, refer to the applicable pages in the math chapter of a full-blown textbook.

All of the math questions will be about items a licensee ***might reasonably need to compute in order to <u>provide, confirm, correct, or explain</u> figures in the course of a real estate transaction.***

The questions cover issues commonly applied to determining property valuation, buyer financing options, seller proceeds, typical settlement expenses, rental properties, and real estate investment concerns, including depreciation.

These include, at a minimum, the following elements related to property value
- *making adjustments* to a comparable property's sales price
- *determining the price of a subject property* from data on comparables
- *computing replacement or reproduction cost* given the necessary basic price information
- *determining property value* from data related to one of the three approaches to value

Plus, regarding buyer financing, common settlement expenses, and seller proceeds, questions may reasonably address issues such as
- *principal, interest, tax, and insurance (PITI)* totals and sub-parts for impound accounts
- *property taxes*, prorations and determination from assessed value and mill rate
- *property insurance premiums* and prorated portions
- *mortgage insurance premiums (MIP)*
- *title insurance premiums*
- *prorations of prepaid expenses*
- *mortgage interest payments* and *principal balance* at a specified time
- *proration of rents* at closing
- *special assessment charges*
- *brokerage fees*
- *property sales price determinations* from a variable, such as taxes due, commission paid, or a LTV percentage and loan amount
- *buyer's total cost of purchase*
- *seller's net after sale*

Topic Areas A through E will each have 0-2 questions on the exam.

A. Basic Math Concepts

Area

Area computations are most likely to concentrate on determining property square footage *(remember, use the outside dimensions for house and other building square footage, though "living area" computations may be based on interior room dimensions)*, lot sizes, and acreage (43,560 square feet/acre).

Loan-to-Value Ratios

As noted in Topic Area IV-A, loan-to-value (LTV, or L/V) ratios are simply that: the loan amount divided by the value of the property.

LTV ratios divide loan amounts by *the lesser of the appraised value or sales price*, so be careful to avoid using list prices, high sales prices, or other large amounts that might be included in the question's details as an alternative property values.

For example, a property listed for $327,000, appraised at $315,000 and sold for $310,000. If the LTV is 80, the loan amount would of $248,000 (lower of appraisal or sale = $310,000 x 80%).

Discount Points

As noted in Topic Area IV-A, a "point" is one percent of the face value of a loan amount.

Questions about points are most likely to present transaction information and ask either the amount that will be charged for a certain number of points, or what the loan amount is based on a total dollar amount charged for a certain number of points.

Equity

As noted in Topic Area IV-A, equity is the amount of principal a property owner has in a property after deducting liens and claims against it.

Questions about equity are most likely to include elements such as loan amounts, other property indebtedness, appraised value, and list and/or sales prices, and then ask for the owner's equity.

Pre-sale equity is determined using appraised value. Equity calculations based on sales price may vary somewhat if the sales price is close to the appraised value, though a sales price that is much lower than appraised value due to a foreclosure, family member, or estate sale does not present an accurate valuation of the equity.

Also, the proceeds to the seller are not the same as equity, since proceeds are what is left after transaction expenses, such as brokerage fees and prorations, are deducted from the equity a seller manages to get out of a property.

Down Payment/Amount to be Financed

How much money the buyer provides for a *down payment*, sometimes referred to as *earnest money*, is *subtracted from the sales price to give the basic amount to be financed*.

Note, though, that earnest money is generally the deposit that accompanies a purchase offer, and may be supplemented at any agreed-upon time during the transaction by more cash for a larger total down payment.

Each transaction has its own particulars, and questions on the amount to be financed may include variables like "The buyer will also be financing loan fees and other closing costs," and then give the amount(s) to be added to the remaining balance-due for the property itself.

In a scenario like the one above, simply add up all of the payments toward the purchase price to determine the down payment and subtract that from the purchase price for the basic amount to be financed. Then, add any additional expenses the lender will allow to be rolled into the loan to that basic amount to determine the total amount to be financed.

B. Calculations for Transactions, including Mortgage Calculations

Though there are no sub-Topics for this Topic Area, prorations are essential calculations in real estate transactions, and will be defined here despite the term appearing in a Topic Area below.

Prorations are ***proportionate amounts***, or ***apportionments***, of any shared expense, and can either be a credit or a debit to either party. Common shared expenses include taxes, sewer, special assessments, and unused fuel, such as heating oil or bottled gas.

> For example, if a sale includes the buyer reimbursing the seller for 200 gallons of heating oil remaining in a 275-gallon oil tank, the proration would involve determining the current price per gallon then multiplying that amount by 200.

In all real estate transactions, how much money the buyer pays for the property as well as all buyer-paid financing and closing costs is crucial to a successful closing. So expect to see at least one question that lists a lot of expenses and prorations, then asks "How much did the buyer need to close?"

> In most cases, the questions will include all the numbers and information necessary to the math, as well as ***all*** conditions of who pays for what and whether prorations are based on 30-day versus 31-day months and 360-day versus 365-day years.

C. Property Tax Calculations

Property taxes are common in every town, city, and county nationwide, though the method of computing and collecting them are not.

Of all of the Topic Areas in this section, taxation is the most likely to have at least one, if not two, questions, so here's a quick look at basic tax terminology and amounts.

> *You may find that the question(s) present conditions that do not apply in your state, such as referring to an annual bill while yours is billed semi-annually.*

> *Remember, while taking the test you are in "the testing state," not your home state, and all the clues you need should be clearly presented in the question.*

Tax rates are commonly expressed as a ***mill rate***, or ***millage rate***, or ***mills***, which translates into ***one mill = 1/1,000 of a dollar***, or ***1/10 of one cent (.1¢)***.

The tax bill will multiply the mill rate by the assessed value to arrive at the annual taxes due, regardless of whether or not they are paid in installments.

For example, a property assessed at $85,500 in a town with a mill rate of 34.5 will have an annual tax liability of: $85,500 multiplied by 34.5 divided by 1,000, which equals an annual tax of $2,949.75.

> *A quick way to translate the "one mill = 1,000[th] of a dollar" is to just change the comma at the thousand-dollar point in the property's assessed value to a decimal point and multiply that number by the mill rate. So, in the example above, it could be computed as $85.50 times 34.5 equals $2,949.75.*

> ***Practical AND testing note***: *some state taxation systems vary in their use of terms and applications of the basic, common process illustrated above.*

For example, at least one state begins with a property's "fair market value" for taxes, or "tax appraised value," which corresponds to most jurisdictions' "assessed value." This amount is then multiplied by a "tax assessment ratio" of 4% for an owner-occupied primary residence (there are other rates and rules, but they are of no importance here) to arrive at the property's "assessed value." This value, which is MUCH lower than in other states, is multiplied by a mill rate that is MUCH higher.

So, an owner-occupied property with a "tax appraised value" of $200,000 will have an "assessed" value of $8,000, and may have a mill rate for that year of 375. Its tax bill would be $3,000.

For testing purposes, do NOT make any such state-specific adjustments to the basics of assessed value and millage rates provided in a question! If you do, you will NOT find the answer that will get you credit among the choices given, including "none of the above"!

D. Prorations (Utilities, Rent, Property Taxes, Insurance, etc.)
Commission and Commission Splits

These questions will be among the easiest, and are good candidates for a "none of the above" answer.

But the compensation arrangements will be carefully spelled out. Just remember that commission percentages are based on sales price, not on appraised value, loan amount, or seller's net proceeds, and that these three values are commonly used to compute attractive distractors.

One twist on commissions may be to determine sales price based on what the licensee received for a commission. Should you see one of these, simply work backwards, dividing the licensee's compensation amount by the prorated commission percentage the licensee receives.

For example, if a licensee earns $18,000 on a 30% share in a 6% brokerage commission, the licensee's $18,000 is 1.8% of the sales price, or $18,000/.018 = $1,000,000.

Seller's Proceeds of Sale

Sale proceeds are the heart and soul of a real estate transaction, so expect to see at least one question that includes a variety of transaction details, then asks "How much did the seller make on this sale?"

These questions may require you to make several calculations from other areas and combine them to get the "bottom line" for the seller, or a prorated amount for a party with a specified interest in the sale.

For example, three heirs to a property may have a 50 percent, 25 percent, and 25 percent interest, respectively, and the question may ask how much the first heir will receive from the sale proceeds

Transfer Tax/Conveyance Tax/Revenue Stamps

Taxes paid on property sales vary from place to place, as do what the taxes are called.

Questions on these taxes will include all necessary variables. As noted in the Topic Area on taxes above, you are in the "testing state," not your home state, so answer the question based solely on the information, and names, provided.

Amortization – Interest Rates – Interest Amounts – Monthly Installment Payments

This area commonly focuses on total payment amounts as well as individual components. Questions will provide the necessary variables for calculating such amounts as

- *principal portion* of a monthly payment
- *interest portion* of a monthly payment
- *total monthly payment* given a particular interest rate and annual charges for taxes and property insurance *(PITI – principal, interest, taxes, and insurance)*
- *reserve, or impound, or escrow amounts* held by a lender based on the variables presented, such as a particular percentage of annual taxes and property insurance
- *mortgage insurance premiums (MIP)* charged for loans with an LTV over 80%
- *remaining principal* given the interest rate, term period, and number of payments already made

Refer to your primary text for explanations of how to perform these mortgage calculations, and remember that you may not even get a single question from this area.

Buyer Qualification Ratios

These questions will provide variables such as buyer income, savings, and other resources and then ask how much a buyer can afford to either borrow or pay per month for a mortgage.

The critical elements needed to compute these amounts will be provided, so read any question on qualifying buyers carefully to make sure you *use only* the applicable factors when computing the *maximum loan amount or monthly payment* a buyer can afford.

The following *ratios* are applicable to buyer qualification, and may be tallied in Topic Area IV-A, Financing, General Concepts, if they are about the basics, or in this Topic Area if they involve computations.

- *debt-to-income (DTI) ratios*, or simply *debt ratios*, which refer to the percentages of a borrower's gross (pre-tax) income that will be allocated to monthly debt obligations; there are two main kinds of DTI
  - *house expense, front, or front-end, ratio*, which refers to *just the housing expense* (mortgage payment) *divided by gross income*—for example, if a property's monthly PITI payment is $1,100 and the prospective borrower's monthly gross income is $4,000, the *front-end DTI is 27.5%*
  - *total debt, back, or back-end ratio*, which refers to housing expense plus recurring debt (credit cards, car loans, student loans, etc.) divided by gross income—for example, if the same prospective borrower grossing $4,000 has $400/month in recurring debt, the *total* monthly debt obligation would be $1,500 and the *back-end DTI would be 37.5%*
    - *DTI ratios* help lenders *gauge their risk* by seeing how much of a financial cushion borrowers have between what they earn and what they will owe; the front-end shows them what an otherwise debt-free borrower has, while the

> *back-end shows them the "current reality" of a borrower, and how "close-to-the-bone" they are—a few unexpected $1,000 car repairs or doctor bills could put the lender's payments in arrears!*

> • . *Lenders tend to conform to certain upper limits on each ratio, though **the total debt ratio is the ultimate "line in the sand."** For example, an FHA web posting noted in 2013 that "FHA maximum debt to income ratio is 54.99%. Most lenders will limit maximum debt-to-income to under 50% and some lenders to 45%."*

After taking all of the applicant's financial data and processing it, the lender will make a determination on the amount of money it will lend to the applicant.

This may be a ***formal written commitment*** or it may be a ***qualified*** or ***conditional approval***, which means that it is more concrete than a preliminary commitment, but probably stops short of being legally binding.

A conditional approval rather than a binding commitment would be prudent from the lender's position, since lenders prefer to reserve the right to respond to changes in property values or borrower finances.

E. Calculations for Valuation
Competitive/Comparative Market Analyses (CMA)
As noted in Topic Area III-C, CMAs are similar to appraisals, but with a lot of shortcuts.

Questions on this topic will use a licensee's preparation of a CMA as a way of applying the principles of the appraisal process either to specific elements of a property's value or to determining a recommended listing price.

A common source of questions in this area is adjusting the value of comparable properties to arrive at the value of a subject property – remember to add and/or subtract the value of a comparable property's differences to the comparable's sales price, not to the subject property.

Other appraisal principles tested here may include determining (1) the cost of an improvement, such as replacement carpeting or paint, (2) an outbuilding's value based on per-square-foot replacement cost, and (3) a recommended listing price after reviewing details of several comparable property sales.

Net Operating Income
This topic will most likely include questions on rents, expenses, and investment returns associated with both residential and commercial properties; these questions will provide all of the details you need to answer them.

The question you may see will probably focus on a common income property issue like (1) ***gross rental revenue***, (2) property manager or licensee's ***compensation***, (3) owner or investor's ***return on investment***, or (4) ***rental rates based on factors such as square footage and type of lease***.

Other questions that might appear in this Topic Area could present information related to determining such matters as *occupancy rates, gross income determinations, property manager's income, property capitalization rate, owner's taxable income, general budget review, or net operating income (NOI).*

The following *three categories of income* are important to remember for rentals and other investment properties. *The last of these is the one to use for computing cap rates.*

- *potential gross income*, or *projected gross income*, or *scheduled gross income*, which means the *maximum rental income* at 100 percent occupancy
- *effective gross income*, which means the *actual income* after subtracting vacancies and rent collection losses
- *net operating income (NOI)*, which is *what's left of the effective gross income after subtracting all of the property's operating expenses*, such as maintenance, taxes, insurance, reserves for replacements, and other recurring expenses (but not debt service, such as mortgage interest)

Depreciation

This topic will most likely include questions based on a set of property depreciation variables given in the question.

Any depreciation computation will most likely be a component of a CMA/appraisal question, asking you something like, "If property values in a particular subdivision have been declining by an average of 4.9 percent annually, how much should a licensee preparing a CMA depreciate a comparable property sale that is eight months' old?"

Capitalization Rate

As noted earlier, to *compute the capitalization rate* for a particular property, simply *divide the property's net operating income by its price*.

- For example, a $200,000 property that has a $20,000/year net operating income has a capitalization rate of 10 percent.

To *estimate a property value from a cap rate*, analyze several recent comparable sales to determine their cap rates, develop an appropriate composite cap rate for the subject property, then *divide the subject property's NOI by the cap rate*.

- For example, if an area's market currently supports a cap rate of 5 percent and the NOI for a property is $10,000, the estimated property value would be $200,000.

Gross Rent and Gross Income Multipliers (GRM, GIM)

Another income approach method of estimating value is the *gross rent multiplier (GRM)*, or *gross income multiplier (GIM)* method.

Using recent sales, *divide each comparable property's sales price by its gross income, either monthly or annual*, using the same time-period standard (monthly/annual) for all, to determine their respective GRMs.

Then, after developing a representative GRM from a reconciliation of the collective GRMs, *multiply the subject property's income by the GRM* to arrive at a general estimate of value.

- For example, if there is a GRM of 135 for monthly rents in an area, and a property has a monthly rent of $1,200, the property's value would be expected to be around $162,000.

Finally, remember these points as you go into the test

- *If you miss <u>all and only</u> the math questions, you would score 92% on the test*
- *If you miss <u>all and only</u> the math questions, you would still be at least 15 points above the pass/fail line*
- *It is highly unlikely that you will get more than two questions from any Topic Area*
- *It is highly likely that you will get NO questions from one or more Topic Areas*
- *Most of the six math questions on the test are not particularly complicated*
- *Those that are simply require you to take a deep breath and think a little harder*
- *Expect the questions themselves to provide all the numbers and information necessary to do the math*
- *You should be able to at least rule out a few of the answer choices and then be able to make a better-odds guess at whatever's left*
- *"Mark" any question you need to spend time on, then come back to it*
- *Leave no question unanswered: pure guessing gives you 1 out of 4 odds, which translates into at least one correct/credited answer out of this group of six*

<u>*This ends the presentation of key terms and concepts likely to be either tested or used as distractors in this Content Outline Section.*</u>

XI-A. Subdivisions, including Development-wide CC&Rs
(Expect 0-2 questions from this area)

Property subdivisions require the subdivider to comply with all applicable regulations regarding lot size, utility and water lines, street construction, and many other details, which are often simply called *mapping requirements*, in order to be able to get the plan approved, recorded, and underway.

As noted above in Topic Area II-D, Private Controls, *subdivisions are typically created with a list of private restrictions* often known as *subdivision covenants, conditions, and restrictions (CC&Rs)* or *owners' association rules*, or *HOA rules*, that encumber the use and/or transfer of property.

Private restrictions generally seek to accomplish similar ends, such as allow or disallow pets in a subdivision, or clarify where to put trash and recyclables, regardless of which of the following names they may use. Depending on the property type and local conventions for terminology, they may be referred to as

- *deed restrictions*
- *restrictive covenants*
- *covenants, conditions (or codes), and restrictions (CC&Rs)*
- *condominium owners' association rules* for condominium-specific restrictions
- *homeowners' association rules* for subdivision-specific restrictions

Private restrictions are often more restrictive than local zoning ordinances, which means they may either *enhance or detract from property values*.

Private restrictions on land use are *contractual rather than statutory* and are prepared by *subdivision developers* as well as *individual property owners* to limit the use of a property by future owners. For example, a *developer* may sell lots with restrictions on building styles or property uses.

CC&Rs, as well as most other enforceable deed restrictions, *are generally available in the public record*; a *court injunction may be required to stop violators*.

Note, however, that *illegal restrictions, such as those that violate federal Fair Housing laws, are not enforceable*.

XI-B. Commercial, Industrial, and Income Property (Expect 0-2 questions from this area)

Although you will not see more than two scored questions from this Topic Area, *commercial real estate* is a distinct, significant, and often quite lucrative category within the real estate profession.

Often those who choose to practice commercial real estate focus solely on commercial projects and refer all residential real estate to other licensees.

If you are planning on getting into residential work, it would be wise to make some friends in the commercial area, since they often have lots of referrals when one of their projects results in business relocations.

Also, many commercial agents find a niche, like recreational facilities, marina projects, manufacturing or warehouse businesses, or finding sites for franchise food chains, and refer other commercial projects to a colleague.

Though residential listings may take months to move from a listing to a closing, commercial projects commonly take years. Extra time is required for such development-specific complexities as aggregating separate properties, generally through purchase options, to create a large enough site for, say, a mall or "big-box" store, and then helping schedule and receive local zoning approvals and building permits to allow the development to proceed.

In short, the necessity of constant close contact with corporate executives, commercial lenders, legal and accounting professionals, local landowners, and municipal planning and zoning departments calls for detail-oriented candidates with extreme patience, an entrepreneurial vision for new ventures, and the financial wherewithal to last a long time between commission checks.

Commercial property generally involves a variety of **corporate and business ownership structures** that are typically more intricate than others presented in this book.

For office buildings, professional complexes, and other commercial ventures, there are a variety of **partnerships**, such as a **syndicate**, **joint venture**, **limited liability corporation (LLC)**, and more, that are simply too sophisticated for entry level agents to either encounter or be expected to know in detail.

However, the following **three categories of income** are important to understand for commercial rentals and other industrial, income or investment properties, especially since they have direct application to math in Topic Area X-E, Calculations for Valuation
- **potential gross income**, or **projected gross income**, or **scheduled gross income**, which means the **maximum rental income** at 100 percent occupancy
- **effective gross income**, which means the **actual income** after subtracting vacancies and rent collection losses
- **net operating income (NOI)**, which is **what's left of the effective gross income after subtracting all of the property's operating expenses**, such as maintenance, taxes, insurance, reserves for replacements, and other recurring expenses (but not debt service, such as mortgage interest)

The following five sub-topics are listed on the outline as relevant to this Topic Area, so even though they have been treated adequately elsewhere, they will be noted here, where they may be tallied.

- **Trade Fixtures**

  Fixtures, mentioned in Content Area I, are of special importance in commercial, industrial, and income properties. Generally, anything a residential tenant **attaches** to a rental unit in a permanent manner can be argued as becoming real property and thus must be left in the unit at the end of the lease period. **Trade fixtures** are more commonly understood to remain the tenant's property, though all tenant-provided **improvements**, both residential and commercial, should be spelled out as **owned or leased inclusions** to avoid confusion.

- **Accessibility**

  The **Americans with Disabilities Act (ADA)** apply to **public building and workplace access and other accommodations** for those with disabilities.

  Since commercial and income properties involve a wide variety of public **retail and business properties**, the provisions of ADA especially affect owners and landlords by making them responsible for such access concerns as designated parking, curb and building-entry ramps, elevators, automatic doors, larger rest room stalls with grab bars, and lower public telephones.

• Tax depreciation

This is an area that shouts out to licensees, "Tell clients to seek professional advice from an accountant or tax attorney!" Nevertheless, some general information is always useful. In short, there is a standard accounting practice of computing property value depreciation and plugging it into tax returns as a deduction. Every project will have its own set of buildings, land, and equipment that will be reviewed by a tax professional for its depreciation value in tax returns.

• 1031 exchanges

As noted previously, another matter that is of common concern to investors in all types of properties are *1031 exchanges*, named for the IRS Code Section 1031, which afford investors the opportunity to *reinvest funds from a property sale in like-kind properties* and thereby *defer* their accumulated *capital gains tax liability.*

For example, a person may have bought a house as a primary residence twenty years ago for $200,000 and moved out-of-state ten years ago, turning the property into a rental. If the property is sold today for $500,000, the owner's tax liability for capital gains of $300,000 may be deferred indefinitely by purchasing another residential rental property for $500,000.

*Not surprisingly, 1031 exchanges have a whole set of rules, such as a **time limit for qualifying reinvestment purchases (45 days to identify potential replacement property; 180 days to buy it)** and numerous accounting details, and all must be met for the above scenario's new property to qualify as a reinvestment. The rules are too complex for entry-level licensure testing; some regulators would argue that even simple definition questions on this topic should only be used on broker exams.*

However, since 1031 exchanges are not uncommon in practice, you should be familiar with the basic concept. Besides, the term may appear as a distractor!

Boot *is another term commonly associated with 1031 exchanges for **additional cash** required over the reinvestment amount from sold properties. However, it typically refers to any cash or other goods added to any transaction to make up for differences between a new property's value and funds available from a sold/exchanged property.*

Special reminder: to limit your liability as well as ensure greater accuracy, refer clients to an accountant or tax attorney for answers to tax-related questions.

• Trust fund accounts for income properties

Commercial property generally involves a variety of *corporate and business ownership structures* that are typically more intricate than others presented in this book.

For office buildings, professional complexes, and other commercial ventures, there are a variety of *partnerships*, such as a *syndicate*, *joint venture*, *limited liability corporation (LLC)*, and more.

Each of these requires complicated accounting, and if a licensee is managing trust funds for any property management ventures, the applicable trust account guidelines and regulations would be promulgated and enforced by the state; the only general questions on this sub-topic would rely on the fiduciary principle of accounting.

This ends the presentation of key terms and concepts likely to be either tested or used as distractors in this Content Outline Section

THE SAMPLE EXAM BEGINS ON THE FOLLOWING PAGES

Test Tips Page

A Few Test-Taking Tips

The exam-prep power of each question will be multiplied as much as four-fold if you make sure you know the meaning of the wrong answers, or distractors, as well as the correct one.

Distractors are generally written using
- terms and concepts from the same category as the correct answer
- common misconceptions, misunderstandings, or mistakes
- information that is incomplete, overly complete, or correct for a different, closely-related reason

So remember – when reading the questions, and especially when reviewing your answers, pay special attention to the distractors: *Many of them will be used as the "real" answers on the real exam!*

Some of the points made regarding math questions earlier in this book are true for all questions, such as
- "Mark" any question you need to spend time on, leaving its answer choices blank, then come back to it – something in a later one may loosen your mental log-jam
- Leave no question unanswered when you consider yourself finished with the test:
  - *Pure guessing gives you 1 out of 4 odds*
- However, you should be able to rule out at least a few of the answer choices, and then be able to make a better-odds guess at whatever's left
- You get to miss questions and still pass: and *you get to miss a lot*—20 or more!

Finally, remember these Math-Specific points as you go into the test

- If you miss only the math questions, you would still score over 90% on the test
- Most of the six (6) questions on the test are not particularly complicated
- Those that are simply require you to take a deep breath and think a little harder
- Expect the questions themselves to provide the numbers and information necessary to do the math

After completing and scoring the following questions, remember that even if your scores are strong, you should review all of the questions to make sure you also understand the terms and concepts presented in the distractors.

Now get out that scratch paper and begin reading and answering the following questions. Good Luck!

1. Which of the following statements BEST defines real property?
   1. Land and the air space above it.
   2. Land and its improvements and all included ownership rights.
   3. Property that has been surveyed and identified by a full legal description.
   4. All of the rights to land and improvements as identified in a property deed.

2. Residents of an area with wells that go dry during severe droughts arranged with the municipality to provide city water to each property. This work is MOST likely to be funded through a
   1. special assessment.
   2. general assessment.
   3. municipal bond for improvements.
   4. grant from the Environmental Protection Agency.

3. Which of the following events will terminate an agency relationship?
   1. Any arrest of the agent.
   2. Bankruptcy of the principal.
   3. Transfer of ownership of the real estate firm.
   4. Violent disagreement between the principal and the agent.

4. A homeowner hires a carpenter to build a back deck and then refuses to pay. The carpenter is entitled to take which of the following actions?
   1. Remove the deck.
   2. Levy a special assessment.
   3. Place a mechanic's lien on the property.
   4. Petition the courts for a partition sale and recover the amount due from the proceeds.

5. When applied to a real estate sales contract, the term "rescission" is MOST likely to indicate that the contract has been
   1. assigned.
   2. recorded.
   3. notarized.
   4. terminated.

6. In the preparation of a competitive market analysis (CMA) or appraisal, which of the following situations is MOST likely to be interpreted as a stigmatizing property condition?
   1. Substandard construction.
   2. The presence of radon gas.
   3. Undiscovered termite infestation.
   4. A history of a major crime on the site.

7. According to the common law of agency, which of the following statements about the fiduciary obligation of confidentiality is CORRECT when an agent represents a principal in a real estate transaction?
   1. It outlasts the termination of the agency relationship.
   2. It must be defined in writing to be legally valid and enforceable.
   3. It is comparable to lawyer/client privilege and cannot be violated.
   4. It applies primarily to information about the principal's finances and motivation.

8. A property deed indicates that the easternmost boundary includes a fifteen-foot right of way allowing owners farther from the main road the right to cross the property. The property across which the others are allowed to pass is known as a
   1. subdivided parcel.
   2. landlocked parcel.
   3. servient tenement.
   4. dominant tenement.

9. A prospective buyer has offered $127,800 for a condominium that appraises at $122,500 and has made a deposit of $5,000. If the buyer arranges a first mortgage of 85% of the appraised value and asks the owner for seller-financing on the difference, how much will that be?
   1. $18,375.
   2. $18,420.
   3. $18,675.
   4. None of the above.

10. Which of the following terms identifies an element that is essential to creating a valid real estate sales contract?
    1. Recording.
    2. Legal purpose.
    3. Title insurance.
    4. Notarized signatures.

11. A couple with a modest combined income and strong employment history is having difficulty qualifying for a conventional loan to purchase a home due to their income and limited cash. Which of the following sources of real estate funding is MOST likely to meet their needs?
    1. Seller financing.
    2. Private investment groups.
    3. The secondary mortgage market.
    4. The Government National Mortgage Association (GNMA/"Ginnie Mae").

12. When preparing a competitive market analysis (CMA), an amenity worth $5,000 in a comparable property is BEST handled in which of the following ways?
    1. It is added to the subject property's estimated base value.
    2. It is subtracted from the comparable property's sales price.
    3. It is disregarded if it represents less than five percent of the comparable's value.
    4. It is averaged over the number of comparables used and added to the subject property.

13. A CORRECT statement about mortgage insurance premiums charged for Federal Housing Authority (FHA) loans is that they
    1. may be included in the total loan amount.
    2. may be paid in single annual installments.
    3. must be returned after the loan balance drops by 10%.
    4. must be paid by the seller for buyers meeting FHA low-income standards.

14. A licensee acting as a buyer's broker is preparing an offer for a buyer, who asks the licensee if there are any tax benefits to arranging seller-financing instead of going to a conventional lender. Which of the following statements represents the licensee's BEST response to this question?
    1. "Seller-financing may be better for the seller than for you."
    2. "I would have to look more closely at the other variables before I can give you an accurate answer."
    3. "The tax consequences of different kinds of financing do not vary greatly enough to worry about it."
    4. "Make your best offer and include a contingency allowing you to review your options with a tax accountant or tax attorney."

15. Which of the following types of buyer-broker agreements provides the licensee with the GREATEST assurance of receiving compensation if the buyer purchases a property?
    1. Nonexclusive agency.
    2. Open buyer agency.
    3. Exclusive-agency buyer agency.
    4. Exclusive buyer agency.

16. A property owner built a house on a 7,500 square foot lot several years prior to the enactment of new zoning that requires at least 20,000 square feet for residential properties in that area. A CORRECT statement about this situation is that the
    1. property represents a nonconforming use and nothing must be done.
    2. municipality must grant a variance to this property and others like it.
    3. title will have a cloud on it that must be removed prior to any future sale.
    4. owner must purchase additional neighboring property to be in compliance.

17. A property owner on a private road objects to a new neighbor's choice in erecting a white vinyl fence, saying it is ugly and violates the traditional neighborhood balance of stone walls and hedges. Under which of the following circumstances could the fence be prohibited and its removal required?
    1. A majority of all owners within 150 feet of the new fence vote for its removal.
    2. The previous owner records a notarized affidavit attesting to the traditional aesthetic.
    3. There is either a deed restriction or HOA in place that requires only natural fencing.
    4. None; owners of private property cannot be restricted in their choice of home security.

18. Requirements governing which real estate transaction records must be kept and for how long are determined PRIMARILY by which of the following authorities?
    1. Federal law.
    2. Local convention.
    3. Company policy statements.
    4. State regulations and related rules.

19. A buyer arranges for a $90,000 mortgage loan with an annual interest rate of 8% and a fixed monthly payment of $745. If the first loan payment is due 30 days after the loan origination date, how much of that payment will represent principal? (Use a 360-day year and 30-day months.)
    1. $125.
    2. $145.
    3. $600.
    4. None of the above.

20. A homeowner without any liens on the property arranges for a loan that provides a series of small monthly payments to the owner rather than a single large payment that must be paid back in installments. This arrangement is BEST identified as which of the following types of loans?
    1. Blanket.
    2. Open end.
    3. Home equity.
    4. Reverse annuity.

21. Shortly after taking a property listing, the listing licensee is approached by a family member who asks the licensee to prepare an offer at a significantly reduced price. Under the common law of agency, the licensee MUST
    1. refuse to prepare or present this offer.
    2. attempt to get the relative to match the list price.
    3. discuss the potential conflict with an attorney prior to proceeding.
    4. disclose the family relationship with the potential buyer to the seller.

22. A licensee showing some properties to a client-buyer only selects properties in areas where the owners are of the same general age, sex, and ethnic background as the client-buyer. According to federal Fair Housing law, this conduct would be an example of an illegal practice known as
    1. steering.
    2. redlining.
    3. panic peddling.
    4. property stigmatization.

23. A residential property owner wants to buy a vacant lot next to the property to build a garage and small guest house. The lot has a recent appraisal of $10,000, but the property owner is prepared to pay more than that, if necessary, to be able to expand. Which of the following terms BEST identifies the amount the owner is willing to pay?
    1. Market price.
    2. Market value.
    3. Assessed value.
    4. Actual cash value.

24. When a property's creditors are not fully repaid out of the proceeds of a foreclosure sale, they may make a foreclosed property owner personally liable for the balance due by bringing a legal action for a
    1. property lien.
    2. deficiency judgment.
    3. satisfaction of mortgage.
    4. deed in lieu of foreclosure.

25. Which of the following terms identifies a property owner who has entered into an agency relationship with a licensee?
    1. Proxy.
    2. Vendee.
    3. Principal.
    4. Fiduciary.

26. A couple asks their buyer agent which way to take title so that a surviving spouse will inherit the other person's interest even without a will and the agent says, "Joint tenancy with the right of survivorship is the way you want to go." In this situation, the agent's response is BEST described as
    1. sound advice.
    2. misrepresentation.
    3. illegal practice of law.
    4. valid only in community property states.

27. As used in property management, the term "constructive eviction" is BEST understood to mean that a
    1. landlord is building a case against a tenant for eviction.
    2. court has made public its decision to support an eviction request.
    3. property has been sold and the tenant has been paid to vacate the premises.
    4. tenant has left a property after a landlord has allowed it to become uninhabitable.

28. In performing a direct sales comparison (market data) analysis, an appraiser would be MOST interested in data on
    1. comparable properties.
    2. current cost of building materials.
    3. demographic changes in the community.
    4. local economic forces and population trends.

29. During an appraisal of a residential property, an appraiser estimates the cost of rebuilding the subject property so that it is identical to its current size and condition. This is an example of which of the following appraisal principles?
    1. Balance.
    2. Conformity.
    3. Substitution.
    4. Anticipation.

30. An appraiser determines that a subject thirty-year-old residence has a replacement cost of $185,000 and is on a parcel of land worth $47,000. The structure's accrued depreciation from physical deterioration and functional obsolescence is estimated at approximately 40%. Given this information, which of the following BEST represents the property's value?
    1. $139,200.
    2. $158,000.
    3. $232,200.
    4. None of the above.

31. Which of the following statements BEST defines what is meant by the term "material defect"?
    1. Any condition that may change a principal's mind about buying or selling.
    2. Any property defect that would cost more than 10% of the sales price to correct.
    3. All conditions that add to a property's overall structural deterioration or depreciation in value.
    4. All factors that the seller would prefer prospective buyers not to know about the seller's motivation.

32. A buyer-broker agreement is MOST likely to create which of the following types of agency relationships?
    1. Dual.
    2. Single.
    3. General.
    4. Universal.

33. Which of the following government powers provides for the transfer of ownership of real property from an owner to the State in the event the property owner dies without a will or known heirs?
    1. Escheat.
    2. Taxation.
    3. Police power.
    4. Eminent domain.

34. Which of the following statements BEST defines what a "time is of the essence" clause means in a real estate sales contract?
    1. The contract provisions must be met in a timely fashion.
    2. The contract is subject to cancellation if any time requirement is not met.
    3. Any party that breaches the conditions of the clause is liable for liquidated damages.
    4. The conditions of the clause must be satisfied within forty-eight hours of acceptance or the contact becomes void.

35. A person who owns a house in severalty dies intestate. This person's spouse has also passed away, and one of their three children ran away from home and has not been heard from in over twenty years. Which of the following statements about the transfer of this property is CORRECT?
    1. The property will escheat to the state since the owner died intestate.
    2. The two known children will receive a life estate interest in the property.
    3. The three children will be named as joint tenants with right of survivorship.
    4. The missing child represents a cloud on the title for future property transfers.

36. Which of the following situations BEST exemplifies an implied agency relationship?
    1. A new licensee becomes affiliated with a firm and begins hosting open houses.
    2. A seller expresses an interest in finding a similar property in a neighboring town and the listing licensee brings the seller to see some in-house listings.
    3. A prospective buyer becomes quite friendly with the listing licensee during an open house and agrees to see other listings even after declining to sign a representation agreement during that meeting.
    4. A licensee who has been going to a particular physician for over five years is hosting an open house and the physician comes in and talks with the licensee at length about property details and the neighborhood.

37. Which of the following documents creates and identifies the extent of authority for a property manager acting on behalf of an owner?
    1. License law.
    2. Local zoning laws.
    3. Management agreement.
    4. Federal and state civil rights statutes.

38. The use of which of the following construction materials is specifically banned by federal law?
    1. Oil-based paint.
    2. Lead-based paint.
    3. Fiberglass insulation.
    4. Styrofoam insulation.

39. According to the statute of frauds, in order for real estate sales contracts to be enforceable in court they MUST be
    1. recorded.
    2. witnessed.
    3. in writing.
    4. between competent parties.

40. If the advertising statements below about why to chose one real estate firm over another were accurate, which one would represent a violation of the Sherman Antitrust Act?
    1. "We work harder than any other firm to earn your business now, and welcome you back later!"
    2. "No other agency will give you the same level of attention, including researching the best neighborhood for you."
    3. "We search for bargains, unlike others that waste your precious time walking through unaffordable properties."
    4. "With buyer-broker commission rates the same all over this country, we simply give you more 'bang for the buck'!"

41. The provisions of the Americans with Disabilities Act (ADA) are MOST likely to apply to owners of which of the following types of property?
    1. Condominiums.
    2. Time-share properties.
    3. Single-family residences.
    4. Multiplex movie theaters.

42. Which of the following ownership interests applies to parties who own real property as tenants in common?
    1. The ownership interests must be equal.
    2. The ownership interests may be conveyed separately.
    3. The last surviving owner gets title to the property in severalty.
    4. The ownership interests may not be transferred by will or intestate distribution.

43. Which of the following situations BEST characterizes a property suffering from external (economic) obsolescence?
    1. A car dealership is located downwind of a new hog farm.
    2. A house loses value due to leaking gutters and old wiring.
    3. A school building is discovered to have asbestos problems.
    4. A shopping center has an anchor tenant that goes bankrupt.

44. Which of the following types of leases provides for the tenant to pay a base rent and some of the property expenses, such as utilities, maintenance, and taxes?
    1. Net
    2. Index
    3. Gross
    4. Graduated

45. A listing licensee discovers the listed property has a history of faulty plumbing that has never been adequately corrected. The licensee's responsibility regarding this information is that the licensee MUST
    1. include a reference to the plumbing in all advertising.
    2. disclose it only if asked directly by a prospective buyer.
    3. discuss it with the seller and disclose it to prospective buyers.
    4. treat it as confidential and disclose it only with the permission of the seller.

46. The type of legal description that refers to a point of beginning, may refer to monuments, and uses distances and directions to come back to the point of beginning is
    1. lot and block.
    2. metes and bounds.
    3. vertical land description.
    4. government rectangular system.

47. A developer approaches a municipality with a plan to purchase an available lot in a growing neighborhood if they will allow it to be used for a combination laundry and convenience store. Which of the following characteristics of value is MOST apparent in this developer's plan?
    1. Utility.
    2. Scarcity.
    3. Demand.
    4. Transferability.

48. The Sherman Antitrust Act specifically prohibits which of the following activities in the course of a real estate transaction?
    1. Usury.
    2. Price-fixing.
    3. Refusal to return earnest monies.
    4. Failure to disclose property defects.

49. At the time it is signed by all required parties, what type of a contract is a real estate option contract?
    1. Void.
    2. Implied.
    3. Bilateral.
    4. Unilateral.

50. A prospective buyer and an agent prepare an offer. The seller reviews the offer and accepts it with the added provision that the earnest money will be forfeited by the buyer if the buyer backs out for any reason. Which of the following statements about this situation is CORRECT?
    1. There is a binding contract on the property.
    2. The prospective buyer is obligated to the terms but the seller is not.
    3. The seller has legally rejected the original offer and replaced it with a counteroffer.
    4. The provision about the earnest money is not an essential part of a valid contract and violates the statute of frauds.

51. Which of the following interests in real property does a prospective buyer receive once an offer to purchase becomes a binding offer?
    1. Possession.
    2. Ownership.
    3. Equitable title.
    4. Right to encumber.

52. A licensee takes an "as-is" listing on a residential property downhill from an abandoned industrial site. The licensee finds a buyer for the property who discovers after closing that residual industrial waste has been leaching into the house's water supply for several years. In this situation, which of the following parties is MOST likely to have liability for the expense of correcting this problem?
    1. The new owner only.
    2. The industrial property's owner only.
    3. The former residence owner and the licensee only.
    4. The industrial property owner, the former and the current residence owners, and the licensee.

53. When a deed or a lien is placed in the public records in order to make them available to anyone searching the records, this is known as
    1. recording a lis pendens.
    2. recording a satisfaction piece.
    3. providing actual notice.
    4. providing constructive notice.

54. The terms riparian, accession, and littoral refer to which of the following property rights?
    1. Water.
    2. Mineral.
    3. Logging.
    4. Improvements.

55. Which of the following terms identifies the ownership of real property that is complete and has no restrictions on its use or transfer?
    1. Fee simple.
    2. Abstract of title.
    3. Severalty ownership.
    4. Prior appropriation doctrine.

56. A municipal mass appraisal has assigned a property a fair market value of $306,750. If the municipality has a mill rate of 16.86 and assesses property at 70% of FMV, the annual taxes on this property would be which of the following amounts? (Round to the nearest dollar.)
    1. $1,220.
    2. $2,440.
    3. $3,486.
    4. None of the above.

57. Which of the following general property conditions is MOST likely to be categorized as material?
    1. A small attic.
    2. A cracked foundation.
    3. An exterior in need of paint.
    4. An outdated set of kitchen appliances.

58. Under federal Fair Housing Act requirements, a property manager of a residential multi-unit property may legally refuse to approve which of the following situations?
    1. Allowing a handicapped person to make any accessibility modifications to unit.
    2. Allowing a handicapped person to keep a support animal based on a written no-pet policy that is enforced for all units.
    3. Renting a unit in a property exclusively occupied by persons over sixty-five to a single parent with an infant child.
    4. Renting a unit in a low-rent property to someone whose income is considerably above that of the other tenants.

59. According to the common law of agency, a licensee has which of the following obligations to an individual that prefers to remain a customer rather than become a client?
    1. Confidentiality.
    2. Courtesy and patience.
    3. Honesty and fair dealing.
    4. Only those agreed to in writing.

60. The name of the colorless, odorless gas often found in residential properties that represents an environmental health hazard associated with promoting lung cancer is
    1. radon.
    2. methane.
    3. asbestos.
    4. carbon monoxide.

61. A developer has purchased a 17.3 acre property and intends to subdivide the property into as many building lots as possible. If each lot must be at least 12,500 square feet, and the developer must dedicate a total of 1.7 acres for roads and a subdivision recreation area, what is the MAXIMUM number of lots that can be created on this property?
    1. 44.
    2. 48.
    3. 54.
    4. None of the above.

62. Which of the following appraisal methods would be the MOST appropriate one to use in the valuation of a twenty-year-old post office?
    1. Cost.
    2. Income.
    3. Capitalization.
    4. Direct sales comparison (market data).

63. Access ramps to government buildings, grab-bars in public rest rooms, and a row of pay phones with several placed lower than the others are examples of compliance with which of the following federal laws?
    1. Regulation Z.
    2. Federal Fair Housing Act.
    3. Uniform Commercial Code.
    4. Americans with Disabilities Act.

64. A CORRECT statement about compensation arrangements in real estate agency employment contracts is that they are
    1. determined by application of state regulations.
    2. adjusted periodically by the closest Board of Realtors.
    3. established by negotiation between the seller and the agent.
    4. subject to change if the local housing market fluctuates dramatically during the agreement period.

65. A lender is MOST likely to require a borrower to pay for private mortgage insurance in which of the following situations?
    1. The buyer has a history of bankruptcies.
    2. The property is in an area known for hurricanes.
    3. The lender foreclosed on the property's past owner.
    4. The loan amount is for 90% of the property's value.

66. An unmarried carpenter bought a building lot and erected a two-story home and lived there for three years before selling it for a large profit. According to IRS regulations, what is the MAXIMUM amount of any profit that would be exempt from capital gains tax?
    1. $125,000.
    2. $250,000.
    3. $500,000.
    4. None since the carpenter is a professional builder.

67. The BEST statement about the relationship between a property mortgage and a promissory note is that the mortgage
    1. provides evidence of who made the loan to the property owner while the note identifies the face value of the loan.
    2. provides the details of the installment payments required for the loan while the note creates the legal liability for the repayment.
    3. creates a property lien as security for the note, which gives the details of both the amount of the debt and the terms of repayment.
    4. creates a public record of a property's indebtedness based on the note, which identifies the property location and credit history of the property owner.

68. A lead-based paint disclosure notice MUST be included with a
    1. lease for any property open to the public.
    2. lease for office space for more than 15 employees.
    3. listing agreement for the sale of any historic property.
    4. sales contract for a residential property built before 1978.

69. Which of the following situations BEST exemplifies what is meant by "conversion of funds"?
    1. Using client funds as a source for temporary personal loans.
    2. Depositing an earnest money check in an office trust account.
    3. Disbursing office funds from an operating account to cover routine expenses.
    4. Transferring money from an account at a listing office to one at the selling office.

70. Which of the following statements BEST defines what is meant by "appraised value"?
    1. An estimate of value.
    2. A statement of value.
    3. The most recent determination of market value.
    4. The assessment value of a property adjusted for current conditions.

71. Property managers are often granted a wide range of job-related authority to act on behalf of their principal. This is known as which of the following types of agency?
    1. Special.
    2. General.
    3. Universal.
    4. Subagency.

72. Property taxes for the calendar year are $2,700, payable on December 31, for a property closing on June 15th of the tax year. Which of the following amounts is MOST likely to appear on the settlement statement for prorated taxes? (Use a 360-day year and 30-day months.)
    1. $1,237.50.
    2. $1,350.00.
    3. $1,462.50.
    4. None of the above.

73. Which of the following statements made in a property advertisement is MOST likely to be characterized as puffing?
    1. "Motivated seller!"
    2. "Seller-financing available!"
    3. "New home with plenty of amenities!"
    4. "Best view of the mountains in town!"

74. A property owner lists a residence and specifically avoids telling the listing licensee about a leaking roof. The licensee notices water stains in a closet ceiling, but considers them old and never discusses them with either the owner or the buyer. The property is sold without disclosing this condition and the buyer sues for damages based on material misrepresentation. Do the seller and/or the licensee have any liability? Why or why not?
    1. Neither one is liable because the buyer has the obligation to have the property inspected.
    2. The seller is the only liable party because the licensee was never told about the problem.
    3. The seller and the licensee are both liable because the licensee is responsible for the actions of a principal.
    4. The seller and the licensee are both liable because it is reasonable that the licensee should have discovered this condition.

75. Which of the following types of listing agreements allows a seller to contract with multiple licensees and only compensate the one that produces the buyer?
    1. Net.
    2. Open.
    3. Exclusive agency.
    4. Exclusive right-to-sell.

76. Which of the following documents is used to transfer ownership of personal property that is included in the sale of real estate?
    1. A title.
    2. A bill of sale.
    3. A quitclaim deed.
    4. An original sales receipt.

77. The Truth in Lending Act is a part of which of the following federal laws?
    1. Regulation Z.
    2. Uniform Commercial Code.
    3. Consumer Credit Protection Act.
    4. Dodd-Frank Wall Street Reform and Consumer Protection Act.

78. A property owner who is selling a commercial building at a considerable profit wants to legally avoid paying capital gains on the sale for as long as possible. The seller is MOST likely to achieve this objective by
    1. providing seller-financing to the new owner.
    2. creating a sale-leaseback arrangement with the new owner.
    3. reinvesting the money according to the terms of a 1031 exchange.
    4. getting legal representation and filing for bankruptcy protection immediately after closing.

79. A newly licensed real estate licensee has entered into an independent contractor agreement with a firm's primary broker to work as a salesperson. Under this type of relationship, the firm is MOST likely to be responsible for paying which of the following licensee expenses?
    1. Health benefits.
    2. License renewal fees.
    3. Continuing education course costs.
    4. Office space rent and telephone charges.

80. When acting in a fiduciary capacity for a seller in a real estate transaction, a licensee MUST
    1. be loyal to the seller's interests.
    2. obey all instructions of the seller.
    3. represent no other party in the transaction.
    4. disclose only those facts the seller wants known.

This is the end of the Sample General Exam.

Please check your work closely before turning the page and scoring your answers.

Appendix B: Sample PSI General Real Estate Exam Answer Key and Diagnostic Chart for Analyzing Strengths/Weaknesses

Sample Exam Answer Key & Diagnostic Chart.
Total the Number You Answered Correctly in Each Section and Compare with the Total for that Section.
Math questions, Section X, are further indicated with an *.

#	Key	Sec	#	Key	Sec	#	Key	Sec	#	Key	Sec
1.	2	I-A	21.	4	V-B	41.	4	XI-B	61.	3	X-A*
2.	1	II-A	22.	1	IX-B	42.	2	I-D	62.	1	III-B
3.	2	V-E	23.	1	III-A	43.	1	III-B	63.	4	IX-B
4.	3	I-C	24.	2	VIII-D	44.	1	VII-F	64.	3	IX-E
5.	4	VII-A	25.	3	V-A	45.	3	VI-C	65.	4	IV-A
6.	4	VI-E	26.	3	IX-F	46.	2	I-B	66.	2	VIII-C
7.	1	V-C	27.	4	VII-F	47.	1	III-A	67.	3	IV-D
8.	3	I-C	28.	1	III-C	48.	2	IX-G	68.	4	VI-A
9.	3	X-B*	29.	3	III-B	49.	4	VII-G	69.	1	IX-A
10.	2	VII-A	30.	2	X-E*	50.	3	VII-E	70.	1	III-B
11.	1	IV-B	31.	1	VI-D	51.	3	VII-D	71.	2	V-A
12.	2	III-C	32.	2	V-A	52.	4	VI-C	72.	1	X-D*
13.	1	IV-C	33.	1	II-A	53.	4	VIII-B	73.	4	IX-C
14.	4	IX-F	34.	2	VII-D	54.	1	I-B	74.	4	VI-C
15.	4	VII-C	35.	4	VIII-A	55.	1	I-D	75.	2	VII-B
16.	1	II-B	36.	2	V-B	56.	4	X-C*	76.	2	VIII-B
17.	3	II-D	37.	3	V-B	57.	2	VI-D	77.	3	IV-E
18.	4	IX-A	38.	2	II-C	58.	3	IX-B	78.	3	XI-B
19.	2	X-B*	39.	3	VII-A	59.	3	V-D	79.	4	IX-D
20	4	IV-B	40.	4	IX-G	60.	1	VI-D	80.	1	V-C

Diagnostic Chart for Outline Area Strength/Weakness Assessment

Outline Area	# Correct	# on Test	% Score
Section I	_____	7	_____
Section II	_____	5	_____
Section III	_____	8	_____
Section IV	_____	6	_____
Section V	_____	10	_____
Section VI	_____	8	_____
Section VII	_____	11	_____
Section VIII	_____	5	_____
Section IX	_____	12	_____
Section X	_____	6	_____
Section XI	_____	2	_____
Totals:	_____	**80**	_____

When reviewing your answers, pay special attention to the distractors:
If you understand them, too, you will be that much more prepared to recognize them as the
CORRECT answer on a "live" test question!

Notes

Notes